Life's Journey
Creating Unitarian Rites of Passage
Daniel Costley

The Lindsey Press
London

Published by the Lindsey Press
on behalf of the General Assembly of Unitarian
and Free Christian Churches
Essex Hall, 1–6 Essex Street, London WC2R 3HY, UK

© General Assembly of Unitarian and Free Christian Churches 2020

ISBN 978-0-85319-093-6

All rights reserved. No part of this publication may be reproduced or transmitted in any form or by any means, electronic or mechanical, including photocopying, recording, or otherwise, without the prior written permission of the publisher.

Designed and typeset by Garth Stewart

Contents

Introduction   v

1   Child-Naming Ceremonies   1
2   Marriage Ceremonies   23
3   Funerals   46
4   Induction of Ministers or Lay Leaders   83
5   Ordination of Ministers   91
6   Membership Services   101
Annex A: Words for Child Namings   107
Annex B: Words for Weddings   119
Annex C: Words for Funerals   127
Annex D: Words for a Membership Service   137
Appendix 1: Wedding Checklist   141
Appendix 2: The Use of Live and Recorded Music in Rites of Passage   143
Further Resources   144
Acknowledgements   146
About the Author   147

Introduction

Rites of passage are the life-blood of a community. They are the ritual marking and recognition of key moments in life – from birth to adulthood, from adulthood to partnership, from partnership to ageing, from ageing to death. Not all lives experience the same sacred points, nor the same moments or experience – although birth and death are standard – yet each of us will go through times of transition and change.

As far back as can be known, humans have taken time to celebrate or mark such stages in life. Be it the birth of an heir, or the death of the family matriarch, there are ancient records of rites being performed within communities. In more recent times, religious communities and authorities have provided the contexts and focal points for rites of passage. The Jewish Brit Milah (circumcision ritual) and Bar Mitzvah and Bat Mitzvah (coming-of-age ceremonies for boys and girls respectively), Christian Baptism, the Hindi Samskaras (life-cycle rituals), and the Sikh Amrit initiation ceremony are all examples of significant moments in an individual's life where they, and the community in which they are grounded, will seek to make public the transition and transformation from one state to another, witnessed by the community and, for many, by God or a supreme Divinity. Alongside these specific rites, the moments when a child is named, a couple are married, and an individual dies are universally marked and celebrated in some way. Rites of passage help to define us, and allow us the opportunity to assume our place in the community, the local area, and the world: to become more aware of our place in time, and the stages of our own life cycle.

In recent times, while attendance at weekly religious services has generally declined, the demand for rites of passage has remained high. Families who would never consider attending a place of worship for a regular service think nothing of asking for a Child Naming, or a

Wedding, or a Funeral with religious overtones. The place of religion and the Divine at these key moments in life remains strong.

Although there is a continuing demand for rites of passage, there is an increasing trend for individuals, couples, and families to seek 'something different' for their service. It may be something less familiar or, perhaps, something more personal. For Unitarians, who for many years have made a virtue of being able to tailor most elements of a rite of passage to meet individual needs, this growing desire for a personal approach has played to our strengths. As a movement without a standard prayer book, and a deliberate refusal to accept dogma or doctrine, we are well placed to offer something unique and appropriate for these important ceremonies.

In 1993, the Lindsey Press published Andrew Hill's book *Celebrating Life*. Now out of print, this was a comprehensive 'book of special services for use in the Unitarian and Free Christian tradition'. It contained draft services for a range of rites, including weddings, baptisms, and funerals, but also ceremonies to mark divorce and to welcome new ministers. Presenting selections of texts that might be used, line-by-line, the book provided, in a good way, a pick-and-mix approach to creating the right service, and it was sufficiently flexible to support original pieces crafted and inserted by celebrants themselves.

Unlike *Celebrating Life*, the book that you are reading now is not so literal in its approach to services, and it does not contain such a large number of suggested texts. Instead, recognising the call for greater guidance on constructing unique rites of passage, and offering the necessary support for celebrants to contribute their own words, this book considers the purpose of each rite, the flow of emotion that the sequence of elements will generate, some indications of possible words and phrasing, and, to encourage difference, some case studies of particular and innovative services conducted by Unitarian ministers and lay leaders in recent times. Creating a unique service, with words from your heart and the hearts of those to whom you are ministering, can be hard, but the results and the difference that they make are incomparable.

There are chapters here on Child Namings, Weddings, Funerals, the Induction of Ministers and Lay Leaders, Ordination, and Congregational Membership. Each chapter concludes with some practical hints, compiled from many different sources, that will help you to create and prepare for a service in a way that will minimise the effects of any unforeseeable errors or changes.

Readers will notice some repetition within chapters, where wording has been duplicated across several variations of a service. This is deliberate. I did not want to produce a book that required users to look back to previous sections for wording, possibly creating confusion about which element went where. Each 'Service at a Glance' is therefore complete in itself, enabling a much easier guide to follow whenever you are preparing a rite of passage. There are Annexes too, containing original words by Unitarians (ministers and others) that might be used in these special services. All have been given freely, and I am grateful for the generosity of all those who have contributed in this way.

As celebrants develop their own style and approach to Rites of Passage, they will begin to draw increasingly on words that they have crafted and used before. Many of the sample scripts in the main body of this book are those that I have written and adapted over several years. There are also words provided by other ministers, as detailed in the acknowledgements. Occasionally, words heard or sourced from other celebrants' services or suggestions will find their way into new approaches. Wherever possible, I have acknowledged this in the text. However, some may remain unintentionally uncredited – something I would wish to resolve in any future edition.

This book is an attempt to be fully inclusive and to recognise the growing and welcome acceptance of all individuals as members of society, of equal worth. All leaders of rites-of-passage services should be sensitive to society's growing awareness and affirmation of transgender language and issues. We must be mindful of the way we use pronouns in worship, and above all we should check how individuals wish to be addressed in terms of the gender titles that they use in everyday life.

I believe strongly that rites of passage are an important and effective way to mark key milestones and transformations in life. These are, literally, life-changing moments. It is incumbent on celebrants, for whom this book was written, to be able to prepare and provide an excellent and tailored service, each and every time. If an individual, a couple, or a congregation feel that they are 'going through the motions' at a rite-of-passage service, then we have failed. This book contains the material to enable you to create your own rites of passage for the twenty-first century.

1 Child-Naming Ceremonies

Introduction

The safe arrival of a child in a family is a cause for celebration. For thousands of years, people have taken time to give thanks, to seek a blessing on the child's life, to seek support for the birth parent(s) and/or guardian(s), and to recognise the start of the new baby's long path to adulthood.

Many religious traditions provide rites of passage to celebrate the arrival of a child, with varying theological and practical interpretations. Many denominations of the Christian Church celebrate child Baptism (also known as Christening), whereby traditionally a child is ritually welcomed into the Church, washed of Original Sin, and protected from the Devil (although some denominations take a softer approach). In the Islamic tradition, children are welcomed in a ceremony known as *Aqiqah*, in which a child is presented to Allah, and donations are made to charity. In Hindu communities a number of special rituals are followed.

Religious ceremonies vary according to geographic location, beliefs, liturgical requirements, scripture, local tradition, and so on. Christian infant Baptism usually involves a sprinkling of water on the baby's head; in Islam and Buddhist traditions, a baby's fine first hair is shaved or cut; in the Japanese ceremony of Oshichiya the child is dressed in white for an intimate naming ceremony, including ornate calligraphic presentation of the new name.

For Unitarians, there is no specific theological or religious requirement for a ceremony to welcome a child. Unitarians do not expect a child to become a member of any religious tradition until they are of an age and competence to make such a decision for themselves. So, our child-naming services are usually an opportunity to give thanks for the birth, to celebrate the new arrival, to seek a blessing and support for the parents or guardians, and to welcome the child into the community.

Unitarian child-naming ceremonies, which for 'traditional' purposes might be known as baptisms, can be held as part of a Sunday morning service or, as is becoming more popular, as a separate service, often on a Saturday or Sunday afternoon. The structure of the service can take any form, but it will often include the use of water in some way, recognising the communal and religious traditions from which Unitarianism has evolved. While usually held in a church, chapel, or meeting house, the ceremony could easily be adapted and held in any location, including out of doors.

It is usual during the ceremony to confirm 'godparents' for the child – most often friends and relations of the family who are willing to play a role in the raising of the child and support the parents or guardians when times are not so good. The term 'godparent' is the one most commonly used, but it is perfectly acceptable to use different terms, such as 'Guide-Parent'. The term used should be acceptable to the parents and those being chosen for the role – and it is for them to confirm to you which title they prefer. The point here is to ensure that our services are inclusive and are able to accept differing approaches to life. One Unitarian minister and her husband were asked to be godparents at an Anglican service. Since he is a Humanist and she a Unitarian, neither felt able to say the words used in the ceremony, and so they regretfully declined the invitation. Instead, they offered to be Fairy Godparents for both children, and they held a separate ceremony to celebrate this more diverse approach.

There are no legal requirements concerning child-naming ceremonies. Such rites are entirely discretionary and separate from the more formal and necessary child registration that is undertaken at the local Register Office after the birth of every child.

You may want to design, or borrow from another Unitarian congregation, a Certificate of Naming (or perhaps Blessing).

This chapter contains suggested Orders of Service for Child-Namings held both as part of a Sunday service and as a stand-alone event. There are also short case studies, written by different ministers, describing their responses to reflect special circumstances. The chapter concludes with a list of 'Top Tips' – short-cut hints for conducting a better service.

Child-naming service at a glance (separate service)

Words of welcome and introduction

An opportunity to welcome the family and friends to the church, meeting house, or wherever the ceremony might be held. A time to explain the purpose of the ceremony (one of welcome and celebration), present the order in which things will happen, and reassure everyone that they will be helped with all words and actions throughout.

Chalice lighting and stillness

For services such as this, people will perhaps have travelled long distances, parents with babies and small children will have undoubtedly scrabbled to get to the church on time, and there will be a need for a disparate group of people to reflect and recognise what brings them all together at this time. This might be a good time to light a chalice or candle and bring everyone to a point of stillness and quiet for a minute or two.

These words by Anna Jarvis might be suitable:

> *Let the flame burn bright, bringing excitement and joy.*
> *Let the flame burn warm, bringing comfort and encouragement.*
> *Let the flame burn high, bringing light and vision.*
> *Let the flame burn for ever, bringing life and love to our world.*

Prayer

The silence might be broken by reflective words or words of prayer, calling on God, or the Spirit of Love, to be present at the ceremony – in our hearts, in our promises, and all around. How this is phrased should be determined through your conversations with the family in preparation for the service: gauge the level of traditional language required, and construct a service with that in mind.

Child-Naming Ceremonies

Child-naming service at a glance (separate service)

Some parents may ask for, or expect, the Christian Lord's Prayer at this point. It is a prayer that many others present might also know, so it might be considered inclusive. It may, however, seem to exclude those who are not from a Christian background. Make these points clear when working with the parents on the format and content of the service, and let their considerations guide the decision on whether to include it.

Hymn or song

A hymn or song provides a good opportunity for the gathering to join together as one. If many of the group are not regular churchgoers, they may find traditional hymns quite hard to follow and sing – although favourites such as 'All Things Bright and Beautiful' or 'Morning has Broken' will often be sung with enthusiasm. Alternatively, popular songs from recent years might be easier to sing (and better known).

Reading(s)

Readings (one, two, or three) may be taken from traditional sources, perhaps from the Bible, or they may be more modern poems or stories. For obvious reasons, children's stories are often popular at these ceremonies, both to capture the attention of children present but also to remind those attending of the importance of a child-like sense of wonder at the world.

Help the parents to determine who might be best to read these passages. It might be appropriate for an aunt or uncle of the child, or perhaps the godparent(s) of the parents themselves. If there is an older sibling, he or she might be able to read. Also, there may be individuals who, if numbers had not been limited, would have been chosen as godparents; this is the perfect opportunity to give them a role too.

Child-naming service at a glance (separate service)

Promises by parents

A welcome to a new child is also a time for public commitment from parents and others to the well-being of the child, and an expression of eternal love for her or him. This is the time to gather parents and godparents around the table at the front, or round a font, or wherever the naming ritual might take place. You might use responsive exchanges such as these:

> SARAH and DEEPAK, you have come here today to declare your readiness to care for your child, REBECCA, in all her needs. This is a solemn and serious responsibility, a commitment that will present challenges, frustrations, and tiredness. Yet it is also a time of great joy and emotional reward.
>
> SARAH, are you prepared to do your utmost for this child's health and well-being, to love her in the face of adversity, and support her through the trials of life?
>
> (Response from SARAH): *I am.*
>
> DEEPAK, are you prepared to do your utmost for this child's health and well-being, to love her in the face of adversity, and support her through the trials of life?
>
> (Response from DEEPAK): *I am.*

Promises by godparents

Again, a time of public commitment. However, for the godparents you might consider a subtly different set of promises – a commitment not only to the child, but also to the parents. Words such as these:

Child-naming service at a glance (separate service)

> JO, MATTHEW, MIRIAM, and JOHN, are you prepared as individuals to offer your support, understanding, and friendship to help NICOLA and ZAK in their endeavours, and to provide understanding and love to this child, THOMAS?
>
> (Response together): *I am.*

Naming ritual

For many, this will be the key moment in the service. Traditionally, this part will involve water poured across the head, or marked on the head with a wet finger, in reference to Christian infant baptism. However, working with the parent(s) or guardians to construct the service, there is nothing to stop you adopting customs from other traditions, or developing your own ideas. For example, you might want to use a flower, to signify beauty, alongside water, and a white cloth with which to dry the child's head if using water, but also to symbolise the purity and innocence of a child.

Whatever you choose to do, ensure that it has been developed with the parent(s) or guardian(s) – this is not the time to spring any surprises. Use this opportunity to develop words, or use existing ones, that bring together ideas of respect, purity, reverence, thankfulness, and promise.

Use the child's full name.

Address

You may wish to offer a short address, or sermon, at this point. This is not essential, and if time is tight or the likely fidgeting of children prevents it, you might agree to skip this element, or at least keep it very short.

Child-naming service at a glance (separate service)

Much of what you might say here should reflect on the positive nature of bringing new promise into the world through a new generation, of which the child is an obvious part. Remind the congregation that the commitments of parents and godparents are serious and solemn promises, made in the presence of others (including, for many, that of God). Balance the solemn promises with the expectation of joy and wonder as the child grows, and the important role that the child will have in helping to shape the world in the future. Humour, brevity, and simplicity are key elements to bear in mind while creating this address.

Blessing

Many parents will ask for a blessing to be given to the child: a calling on the Spirit of God, of goodness and mercy to bless this innocent life. Perhaps something such as this, by Martin Whitell:

> *CONNOR JAMES THOMAS,*
> *may the blessing of light be with you always,*
> *light without and light within.*
>
> *May your mind be filled with wisdom,*
> *And your lips be filled with kindness,*
> *And your heart be filled with love.*
>
> *And may the angels of heaven go with you and protect you all your days,*
> *Bringing you joy and peace and safety.*
>
> *May God bless you and keep you,*
> *May God's face shine upon you, and be gracious to you*
> *And may God give you peace.*

Child-naming service at a glance (separate service)

Reading

Entirely optional, but it may be an opportunity for one of the parents to read a short poem or story to the child, while the child is being held by the other parent, or by a godparent. After the practicalities of the naming ritual, this can be a touching and special moment.

Prayer

Further prayer and reflection on the importance of the service, and of the congregational commitment to the family. Words here might stress the closing of the service, but the opening of the rest of the child's life – influenced and guided by all whom they meet on the way, including those present. Remind the congregation and family of the commitment they are making to help the child take the right path.

Hymn or song

A good way to bring the congregation together as the ceremony draws to an end.

Closing words

An opportunity to thank all for their contributions to the service, including any musicians, readers, and godparents. And special thanks to all the children present for bringing their own good wishes for the baby.

Then a benediction prayer, seeking light, love, and peace for all.

Child-naming service at a glance (included in a Sunday service)

If the service is to be included within a usual Sunday worship service, you will want to reduce the content a little. Introductions, Chalice Lighting, and Readings will all most likely have featured elsewhere in the service. However, it is important to make this element of the larger service special in its own right, and to work carefully with the family in advance to ensure that they feel integral to the service, but also a bit separate and special.

The sections below are the elements of the child-naming ritual that you may wish to include as part of the more regular worship service. It is best to place this element towards the end of the regular service, bringing the closure of both elements together, and enabling parents, guardians, children, and guests to leave when the naming element is completed.

Words of welcome and introduction

A time to explain that the service is being expanded to include a naming ceremony, and to introduce guests (and perhaps family) to the usual attenders. You will also need to say this as part of your introduction to the Sunday service as a whole: make people aware of why there may be guests present, and make them all feel welcome and part of the gathered community.

Candles

Since candles and introductions will have featured earlier in the service, it might be appropriate to consider instead a Candle-Lighting ritual, specific to the child-naming. Such as this by Sheena Gabriel:

Child-naming service at a glance (included in a Sunday service)

> ANWAR and SOPHIE, through your union, this precious new life has been formed. Just as MEGAN carries your genes in her body, so each of you will contribute to the shaping of her heart and mind.
>
> [Light two candles]
>
> These two candles lit before us represent you as individuals, and the strengths and qualities you each bring as parents.
>
> I invite you to light this third candle as a sign of your commitment to work together, in a shared endeavour, for the nurture and welfare of MEGAN.
>
> [Parents light third candle]
>
> And so we pray that the light that shines bright in MEGAN will burn strong for many years to come.

Prayer

A separate prayer to focus on the naming ceremony and the importance of these moments to the child, her or his family, and the wider community.

Promises by parents

A welcome to a new child is also a time for public commitment from parents and others to his or her well-being, and expressions of eternal love for her or him. This is the time to gather parents and godparents around the table at the front, or a font, or wherever the naming ritual might take place. You might use responsive exchanges such as these:

Child-naming service at a glance (included in a Sunday service)

> SARAH and DEEPAK, you have come here today to declare your readiness to care for your child, REBECCA, in all her needs. This is a solemn and serious responsibility, a commitment that will present challenges, frustrations, and tiredness. Yet it is also a time of great joy and emotional reward.
>
> SARAH, are you prepared to do your utmost for this child's health and well-being, to love her in the face of adversity, and support her through the trials of life?
>
> (Response from SARAH): *I am.*
>
> DEEPAK, are you prepared to do your utmost for this child's health and well-being, to love her in the face of adversity, and support her through the trials of life?
>
> (Response from DEEPAK): *I am.*

Promises by godparents

Again, a time of public commitment. However, for the godparents you might consider a subtly different set of promises – a commitment to the child, but also to the parents, in words such as these:

> JO, MATTHEW, MIRIAM, and JOHN, are you prepared as individuals to offer your support, advice, and influence to help NICOLA and ZAK in their endeavours, and to provide understanding and love to this child, THOMAS?
>
> (Response together): *I am.*

Child-naming service at a glance (included in a Sunday service)

Naming ritual

For many, this will be the key moment in the service. Traditionally, this part will involve water poured across the head, or marked on the head with a wet finger, in reference to Christian infant baptism. However, working with the parent(s) or guardians to construct the service, there is nothing to stop you bringing ideas from other traditions, or developing your own ideas. You might want to use a flower, to signify beauty, alongside water and a white cloth.

Develop words, or use existing ones, that bring together ideas of respect, purity, reverence, thankfulness, and promise.

Use the child's full name.

Blessing

Many parents will ask for a blessing to be given to the child: a calling on the Spirit of God, of goodness and mercy to bless this innocent life. Words such as these by Martin Whitell:

> CONNOR JAMES THOMAS,
> *may the blessing of light be with you always,*
> *light without and light within.*
>
> *May your mind be filled with wisdom*
> *And your lips be filled with kindness,*
> *And your heart be filled with love.*
>
> *And may the angels of heaven go with you and protect you all your days,*
> *Bringing you joy and peace and safety.*

Child-naming service at a glance (included in a Sunday service)

Reading

Entirely optional, but it may be an opportunity for one of the parents to read a short poem or story to the child, while he or she is being held by the other parent, or by a godparent. After the practicalities of the naming ritual, this can be a touching and special moment.

Prayer

Further prayer and reflection on the importance of the service, of the congregational commitment to the family. Words here might stress the closing of the service, but the opening of the rest of the child's life – influenced and guided by all whom they meet on the way, including those present. Remind the congregation and family of the commitment they are making to help the child take the right path.

Return to the main Sunday service.

Some alternative naming services

The following are case studies describing services that required some special considerations. They are written by the ministers who prepared and led them, and they reflect their particular approaches. The case studies do not cover every eventuality, but they do provide ideas for how you might respond to your own set of circumstances.

Case Study 1: A Service for an Adult

Although there is a tradition in the United Kingdom, and many other countries, to 'baptise' or welcome babies and children, the basic premise springs from the Biblical story of Jesus, as an adult, being baptised by John in the River Jordan. While there are many subtle meanings and stories associated with the passage, the key point is that Jesus is being purified and welcomed into a new life – of a new commitment to religion, to community, and to helping others. Some of the earlier religious denominations that eventually became Unitarian, such as the General Baptists, were strong supporters of adult baptism as a form of welcome into the community for those who were able to make such a decision for themselves.

While it is currently unusual within Unitarian communities, it is not unreasonable for individuals to ask to be welcomed into a religious community with the purifying water of baptism. In this instance the choices of the person being baptised, or welcomed, rather than the parents or guardian, become key in creating the service. Often a mentor or friend will play an important role, rather than parents. The address also becomes particularly significant, to explain the importance of the faith commitment being made by the individual, the path travelled towards it, and also the role of the worshipping community. Much of the address will be directed to the person being baptised (unlike a child baptism): welcoming, affirming, and encouraging the individual in question.

At one such adult baptism, the man's parents were present but they did not play any specific role, although it was obviously important to warmly welcome them, and other key people attending, who included the man's partner. It was requested that his chaplain-mentor be asked to do a reading, which he did. This baptism took place soon after a main Sunday service – and it was clearly not a 'naming', nor a membership service.

In this particular instance, after an agnostic upbringing, the individual had become a Christian at a liberal Christian gay-friendly church in Birmingham; then he moved to a smaller town a year or so later. Unable to find a gay-friendly Christian church in town, he was recommended to try the Unitarians, which he did, and he stayed. After about a year or so, he requested a baptism.

In this case, the individual was more of a liberal or Free Christian than a Unitarian Christian, and he specifically requested the baptism to be Christian in nature, with specific Biblical readings, a format which could be seen as Trinitarian and was certainly a strong statement of faith. However, similar services could be constructed with less strong connections to Christianity, and a greater emphasis on the renewal and commitment to the Unitarian community or congregation.

Case Study 2: A Celebration of Adoption and Arrival

Rob and David, who were in what was then a Civil Partnership, were a popular gay couple in the city. Their own excitement on hearing that the adoption of a little boy named Martin had been formalised was met with enormous joy in the community. They had attended several naming ceremonies for children of their friends in the local Unitarian church, and so they wondered if the church would be happy to conduct a ceremony for a gay couple who had adopted a very young boy. Plainly we had no problem with this.

In fact it was their suggestion that we make the service more than a naming ceremony: they wanted it to be also a celebration and thanksgiving for the adoption. So we met (they had yet to receive their young son) and we talked through the words that they wanted to say. It turned out to be fairly straightforward to adapt our normal naming format to focus on the new family and their young son.

The majority of their friends were women and mothers, and they decided to have six godparents – all women. They were very keen that just because they were gay men, their son would not be denied the broadest experience of gender. So we agreed to ensure that this was addressed in the words chosen throughout the service.

My normal practice is to include as many as possible of the children present in parts of ceremony, and so, when the day came, the children came to 'bless' the water by making their wishes for Martin as they placed their fingers in the water and collectively chose a flower to use to place the water on his head, his lips, and his chest.

Rob and David came to the front with their son for the part of the service that involved their declaration that they accepted their new child as their own. Then the godparents joined them to give Martin his name, and to share their names with us all before making their promises.

Given the special nature of the occasion, we combined the thanksgiving for birth, the naming, and the affirmation of adoption into one special element:

> ROB and DAVID, Do you receive this child unconditionally as your own?
> We do.
> Will you love him, nurture him, and accept him as part of your family as he grows up?
> We will.
> What family name do you give him?
> (Surname)

> With this water as a sign of purity
> and in the presence of your family and friends,
> I name you MARTIN ANDREW.
> May your mind be filled with wisdom,
> And your lips be filled with kindness,
> And your heart be filled with love.
>
> And may the angels of heaven go with you and protect you all your days,
> Bringing you joy and peace and safety.
> Amen

Case Study 3: A Child-naming When One Parent Had Recently Died

I was asked to conduct a child-naming service for a two-year old boy, Michael, whose father had recently died overseas. The father, Stephen, was a member of the armed forces and had been killed in a roadside ambush.

I spent some time working with Alison, the mother of the child, to ensure that we had a full understanding of the nature of the father's death, the role he had been able to play in the short time that he had known his son, and how we would include his memory on the day.

Alison was clear that she did not want the death to overshadow the day, and that the service was to be a celebration of childhood and parenthood, and the role that extended family and friends play in a child's life. At my suggestion we had a couple of meetings with Alison's mother, to ensure that I was not missing any hidden grief. It was important to meet Alison's wishes and to ensure that there would be few emotional surprises on the day.

The service was separate from the Sunday service, and it followed a fairly traditional format. Recognising that all present would be aware of Stephen's death and the tragedy surrounding the day, we agreed to address this issue early on,. So we began the service with prayers for the loss of Stephen, and the new life that Alison and her son Michael were facing. We made this respectful yet positive, enabling us to move beyond that time, and framing the whole ceremony as a new step forward.

Godparents were expected to play an even more crucial role in Michael's life than would normally be the case. They had been chosen and spoken to with that in mind, which brought an even greater sense of commitment and support than usual.

In conclusion, shaping this service required specific sensitivities concerning Stephen's death, but a necessarily open and honest discussion with Alison as to how this would be dealt with. Not addressing this key element would have deprived the day of an important element of its meaning and its message of hope for the future. Words and songs and ritual seemed to gain a deeper resonance for the family, given the circumstances, yet it was important to remember that the focus for the day was the future, and the celebration of Michael's arrival in the world – not the past.

Case Study 4: An Unexpected Venue for a Naming Ceremony

When I was asked to conduct a baby-naming service in Manchester, I had not expected it to be in a pizza restaurant! The parents had hired the local civic hall for the ceremony and planned to hold the baby's first birthday party in the restaurant next door. At the last minute, they discovered that the hall was still closed for refurbishment. It was hastily arranged with the restaurant that the ceremony would take place there instead.

The restaurant staff had placed the party in two adjoining rooms, off the main restaurant space but without doors. Other diners were enjoying their lunch during our ceremony. We decided to squash everyone into one room, and the archway between the two formed a sort of stage setting.

The ceremony went very smoothly – apart from one point. As with many Unitarian namings, we decided to dip a flower into water and use it to bless the child. Having seen something similar elsewhere, I thought I would involve the other children present by asking them to come forward to bless the water with their good wishes for the baby. No one came forward, so I said 'anyone can come forward', gesturing to one of the guideparents whom I had met before the ceremony. Once a few adults had come forward, most of the guests decided to bless the water, and there was a general mêleé and lots of talking. I knew I had to catch people's attention, and I didn't want to bellow over the crowd, so I decided to sing a verse of a hymn (unaccompanied). The room fell silent, and we were able to continue with the rest of the ceremony.

Case Study 5: Godparent, Guideparent, or Fairy Godparent?

With so many secular or 'spiritual but not religious' people not wishing to have 'too much religion' in the ceremonies, I have noted an increased use of the word 'guideparent' instead of 'godparent'. As a committed Unitarian, my belief is that people should have a personal interpretation of god that is comfortable for them. But obviously some people are not comfortable with the word at all. I was not christened as a child, and so I had a 'Fairy Godmother' in the form of my mother's best friend. She gave me guidance through her knowledge of my family, and the generational gap made her a perfect mentor. Recently, my husband and I were asked to be godparents at an Anglican service. Since he is a happy Humanist and I a Unitarian, neither of us felt that we could say the words used in the ceremony, and so we regretfully declined the invitation. Instead, we offered to be 'Fairy Godparents' for both of our friends' children, and we hope to hold our own ceremony in a park during the summer.

Top tips for child-naming services

Print the order of service on A5 sheets, and place them in an A5, plastic-paged presentation folder. You will be holding the folder with one hand and a baby with the other, so the order of service needs to be manageable and water-resistant.

Don't use roses. If using a flower in the service, try not to use a rose or any other flower with thorns or spikes. Babies will try to grab the flower. Enough said.

Be careful with candles. Keep them well out of reach of children.

Test the bowl or font. If using water in a bowl, test the bowl before the service (ideally not on the day itself). Check that it doesn't leak or allow water to simply drain through a crack (as often happens in rarely used earthenware bowls).

Test the temperature of the water. If using water, try to ensure that it is not too cold: there is nothing worse than a shocked and cross child at the point of naming. Either add a little hot water before the service, or at least ensure that it is at room temperature.

Things will go wrong – you are working with children. It doesn't matter, and if you get cross or frustrated, that will upset the balance of goodwill. Laugh, smile, make a comment, and try to get back on track. People are very forgiving at child-naming ceremonies.

Discourage random photography. There is little more annoying during a service than constant clicking, or phones being held aloft, to 'capture the special moment'. In your introduction, explain why this special and sacred time requires full attention from all and is not enhanced by fiddling about with mobile phones and cameras. If the parents are happy with the idea, try to include a moment after the naming and blessing when photos might be posed.

Get to know the child before the service. You are probably going to hold the child. The child needs to be aware of that, and should preferably have been held by you before.

Involve older siblings. If appropriate, an older sister or brother might be involved in a reading. Or may be asked to hold a flower for the baby, or a special book. Just something to keep them occupied and involved. It's a big day for them too.

2 Marriage Ceremonies

Introduction

A wedding is a celebration of love and a declaration of commitment by two people in front of witnesses – making public their desire to become a 'legal' couple. This legal element can of course be met through either marriage or a Civil Partnership (open to mixed-sex couples as well as same-sex couples with effect from 31 December 2018). For many, the sacred nature of marriage, steeped in tradition and aligned with religious and spiritual connections, will draw them to a church or meeting house to celebrate their union; to declare their love and commitment before a congregation, or before God, is an important element of the ceremony.

Marriage has existed as a sacred bond between couples for thousands of years. It has been an integral part of religious and spiritual traditions for perhaps all of those years, and has evolved over time to reflect changing circumstances. Marriage is a sacrament of the Christian Church and, in the United Kingdom at least, there have been laws and prohibitions around marriage that have been supported by, and sometimes hindered by, the link between church and state. Such ties are much looser now, and weddings can be celebrated in almost all religious traditions and in secular places too.

For Unitarians, the purpose of marriage is generally no different from the way it is perceived by other faiths and secular bodies, although some of the emphasis may be different. Where Unitarians do differ from some, however, is in a willingness to work closely with the couple to develop the service that they seek: we do not use a prescribed prayer book, we have no standard liturgy, and, aside from the latest national legal requirements, the contents of the service can be developed from a blank sheet of paper – realising the dreams of the couple to a large extent.

On the day itself, to lead a wedding service can be a wonderful experience. You are present at one of the most joyous days of the couple's lives; you are making their dreams a reality, and your role can be satisfying and spiritually rewarding.

But despite all the love and happiness surrounding the big day, weddings can be a difficult service to prepare, and to meet the expectations of the couple involved. In current times, the service element of the day will often be competing for attention with the dress, the reception, the flowers, the potential difficulties of family relationships. In addition, many couples have very fixed ideas on how they want the service to run – occasionally counter to a more usual service, or sometimes in a way that experience shows needs careful management.

For centuries, marriage was confined to the union of a man and a woman. In recent years, the law has been revised to recognise the inalienable right of all to declare their love for another and solemnise their relationship. The Unitarian and Free Christian movement, alongside the Liberal Jews and the Quakers, was at the forefront of the successful campaign to allow same-sex weddings to be conducted in religious premises, and this chapter makes no distinction between marriages of two men, of two women, and of a woman and a man. Where appropriate, recognition of any necessary or suggested difference in the service has been included, but only to ensure that the wedding is, as intended, unique and personal to the couple. Note that, at the time of publication, same-sex marriage is still not legal in Northern Ireland.

Understandably, given the legal status of a marriage, there are several formal requirements that need to be met and worked with, both before and during a wedding service. While this chapter will set out some of these issues, it is essential that anyone leading a wedding ceremony, and/or acting as the Authorised Person to declare the marriage legal, understands the legal rules and regulations surrounding weddings in the area where they are conducting the service.

To become the Authorised Person (AP) for your church or meeting house, you must apply to the General Register Office, with the support of Trustees and other Committees. Authorised Persons are authorised only for specific, named venues; although an Authorised Person can be separately authorised for several different buildings, under current rules he or she is not authorised to conduct weddings at unspecified locations.

It will be important, in early discussions, to encourage the couple to attend the local Register Office as soon as possible to ensure that all paperwork is complete and the wedding notices are published in accordance with the law. The couple will need a number of different identity documents to confirm names, nationality, address, marriage status, etc. This process will generally take at least one month, and appointments may take time to be arranged.

In England and Wales, the current rules can be found here: www.gov.uk/get-married-in-england-or-wales

In Scotland:
www.nrscotland.gov.uk/registration/getting-married-in-scotland/how-do-i-go-about-it

In Northern Ireland:
www.nidirect.gov.uk/articles/guidance-marriage-procedures-northern-ireland

In England, Wales, and Northern Ireland, your church or meeting house must be authorised by the Register Office as a place for wedding ceremonies. Note that there is a separate requirement to register for same-sex marriages: existing authorisations to conduct weddings for a man and a woman are not sufficient for same-sex weddings. Furthermore, if you are the Authorised Person for the place, it is essential to read HM Passport Office's Guide for Authorised Persons, to ensure that you are meeting the necessary legal requirements.

The legal nature of a marriage brings with it additional responsibilities for the celebrant. An obvious danger is the opportunity to abuse marriage as a cover to support illegal immigration, or to enable coercive or controlling behaviour. It is essential that the Registrar and minister or celebrant are convinced that the relationship is genuine, and that the couple are truly looking to marry for love and mutual support.

In preparing for the wedding, you will want to take necessary steps to find out more about the couple, their meeting, their background, the stories of their lives. The overwhelming majority of couples will be marrying for the right reasons; very occasionally they will not. If you are concerned about any aspect of the relationship, you must take steps to ask more questions of them, or to discuss your concerns in confidence with another person – ideally the Registrar, if you have serious doubts. As Unitarians, we welcome people of different faiths and beliefs to marry and to prepare for a long wedded partnership; it is your responsibility to ensure that you adhere to the moral and legal obligations that are expected of a minister, celebrant, or Authorised Person.

This chapter contains suggested orders of service for weddings held in churches, meeting houses, hotels, etc. There is a separate section on the use of music. There are also short case studies, written by different ministers, on specific changes that they made to the standard order of service in order to reflect special circumstances. The chapter concludes with a list of 'Top Tips' – essential checks to ensure the delivery of a better wedding service.

Preparation

A wedding is a celebration of love, commitment, and togetherness. It marks a significant transition in the lives of the couple, and history and tradition will be encouraging a happy, intentional, well-choreographed moment in time.

The couple may be known to you, or they may be complete strangers, but your role is the same, from the first time you sit with them to talk through the plans for the day: it is to guide the couple through the possibilities and options for the day, to offer explanations and reassurance, and to work with them to deliver a unique and personal ceremony. Some couples will have definite ideas of how they would like the service to proceed, others will need clear guidance through the basic options. Every couple is different. Make sure you have plenty of time to talk through the options, and take a checklist with you – and one to hand to the couple too. See Appendix 1 on page 141.

Most weddings will involve a number of other people – both before and during the service – including, for example, musicians, ushers, bridesmaids, a best man, and photographers. Their roles need to be borne in mind as you carefully construct the service together.

Your meetings with the couple should help them to understand that the service will be an opportunity for both celebration and sacred reflection. Use the 'Service at a Glance' (below) to guide your questions as you create the service together.

Wedding service at a glance: for a church or meeting house

The arrival

Traditionally, it has been usual for the man, the groom, to arrive at the ceremony first – perhaps at least 15 minutes early – and the woman, the bride, to arrive on time (or a little bit late). The groom will be sitting at the front of the church, usually with the best man. Once the bride arrives, all will stand, and music will play as she progresses to the front of the church, often accompanied by a significant male relative or friend. For many couples, this approach is still favoured – tradition exerts a powerful pull – and can be easily managed.

However, this introduction is not obligatory, and many different approaches can be taken. In the case of same-sex weddings, especially, it is less likely that the couple will want a phased arrival such as this.

Work with the couple to determine how they would like the arrivals to be managed, preferably at a rehearsal and discussion held at the church or meeting house shortly before the big day: they may wish to arrive together; or they may wish to start the service already in place at the front of the church; or they may both wish to arrive and progress to music – as a couple or separately. All these things are possible. If the couple want music, they need to think now about what that music will be – classical? pop? etc. How might the music be played – is there an organist? Or does the church or the couple know another professional musician? Or do they want recorded music, perhaps songs that mean a lot to them as a couple? You may be asked for suggestions, and you may encourage them to listen to traditional wedding marches.

Wedding service at a glance: for a church or meeting house

'Giving away'

In former times, the wedding was a moment where the father of the bride consented to 'give away' his daughter to be married. From a legal perspective, this requirement is long gone – and a good thing too. However, some couples still wish to include such a moment in the service, either to align with tradition or, more meaningfully, to mark a transition from membership of a close family to a new relationship. Some individuals prefer to ask a friend to 'give them away', recognising again the transition from one family and friendship group to a wider one.

Traditionally, words such as these are used:

> *Minister:* Who gives this woman to be wed?
>
> *Father:* I do.

However, recognising progressive changes in our society, you might want to suggest an alternative that retains the traditional structure of the service but adopts a more acceptable, or less traditional, form of words. Although couples might initially prefer the traditional words, once presented with an alternative, many will see this as more acceptable:

> *Minister:* Who accompanies this woman to her wedding? To support her on this day of love, and of commitment to this man?
>
> *Parent/Sibling/Friend:* I do.

It is perfectly acceptable to include such questions and answers for both partners. It is equally acceptable to dispense with this element altogether.

Wedding service at a glance: for a church or meeting house

Words of welcome and introduction

This provides an opportunity to welcome the family and friends to the church or meeting house. A time to explain the purpose of the ceremony (one of commitment, love, and declaration before God and/or family and friends), set out the order in which things will happen, and reassure everyone that they will be helped throughout when particular words or actions are to be used.

Chalice lighting and stillness

People may have travelled long distances to attend the ceremony. They may have had trouble parking. There might be the added pressure of keeping a watchful eye on children. Everyone will feel a sense of relief just to be there. A potentially disparate, unrelated group of people need time to reflect on what has brought them all together. This might be a good time to light a chalice or candle and bring everyone to a point of stillness and quiet for a minute or two.

Some suitable words might be the following:

> *We are gathered here to celebrate the wedding of THOMAS and GERALD. This is an important and sacred time. We need to be focused on these two people, and our time together.*

> *We have travelled from many places to be here today. We should just be pleased we are here, leaving any questions, worries, or concerns to one side.*

> *Let us take a short time in stillness and silence to calm our minds and our bodies, to bring ourselves fully into this place.*

Wedding service at a glance: for a church or meeting house

Declaratory Words

This is a good point, early in the service, for the required 'Declaratory Words' to be said. For a marriage to be legal, the Authorised Person (which may be you) and the witnesses must hear the couple use one of the following declarations:

> *"I do solemnly declare that I know not of any lawful impediment why I, (FULL NAME), may not be joined in matrimony to (FULL NAME)."*

> Or

> *"I declare that I know of no legal reason why I, (FULL NAME), may not be joined in marriage to (FULL NAME)."*

> Or

> *By replying "I am" to the question: "Are you, (FULL NAME), free lawfully to marry (FULL NAME)?".*

Agree with the couple which set of words will be used, and reassure them that they can simply repeat words after you have said them – perhaps dividing the sentence into two or three smaller elements.

Prayer

The silence might be broken by reflective words or words of prayer, calling on God, or the Spirit of Love, to be present at the ceremony – in our hearts, in our promises, and all around. How this is phrased should be determined through your conversations with the couple in preparation for the service: gauge the level of traditional language required, and build a service with that in mind.

Wedding service at a glance: for a church or meeting house

Some family members may ask for, or expect, the Lord's Prayer at this point. It is a prayer that many others present might also know, so it can be inclusive. It may, however, also be experienced as exclusive by those who are not from a Christian background. Make these points clear when working with the couple to prepare for the service, and let their considerations guide the decision on whether to include it.

Hymn or song

A hymn or song provides a good opportunity for the gathering to join together as one. If many of the group are not regular church-goers, they may find traditional hymns hard to follow and sing – although traditional wedding hymns such as 'All Things Bright and Beautiful' and 'Give me Joy in my Heart' are popular and appropriate.

Alternatively, it is increasingly common for couples to choose a favourite and appropriate song for all to sing. The Beatles' 'All You Need is Love' is one such song that is likely to be well known and can be sung by most.

Reading(s)

Readings may be traditional, perhaps from the Bible, or more modern poems or stories may be used. Annex B lists a number of collections of appropriate readings and poems. The internet also provides access to a wealth of appropriate material.

Ensure that you have read through all the readings before the service, suggesting edits or alternatives where necessary.

Help the couple to decide who might be best to read these one, two, or three passages. Many friends and family members will want to be involved. While the couple's first thought might be to invite the best

Wedding service at a glance: for a church or meeting house

man or chief bridesmaid to read, you could gently suggest that there might be others who would appreciate being involved. Are the couple offering opportunities for involvement to as many people as possible? Ultimately, of course, it is a matter for the couple to decide, but they may be grateful to be reminded of the need to include others.

Candle lighting

At this point, the service is turning towards the formal contractual words and vows that will bind the couple, one to another, in law. Working with the couple, consider whether it might be appropriate to include a simple ceremony in which three candles are lit, one by each partner, to celebrate the two individuals marrying, and one to be lit by them both from the first two flames, to symbolise the unity of the couple, and the continued individuality from which they come. Words at this point might include the following:

> REBECCA and SAM, these three candles before us represent the union of your commitment to one another. The two outer candles represent each of you, REBECCA and SAM, as individuals. The third candle, which you will kindle together, represents your marriage, and the progression of your lives in love together. The first two candles will remain lit, however, to show that you also remain as individuals.
>
> (to the congregation):
>
> When the candles are lit, let us spend a few moments in stillness and quiet, to strengthen our focus here today on this wonderful commitment by REBECCA and SAM, declaring their love for one another before you, their friends and relations.

An alternative 'Sand & Glass Box Ceremony' is set out in Annex B of this book.

Wedding service at a glance: for a church or meeting house

Contracting Words

As with the Declaratory Words above, there is a legal requirement for specific 'contracting' words to be heard by the Authorised Person and the Witnesses:

> *"I call upon these persons here present to witness that I (FULL NAME) do take you/thee (FULL NAME) to be my lawful wedded wife/husband.**"*
>
> Or
>
> *"I (FULL NAME) take you/thee (FULL NAME) to be my wedded wife/husband."*

** For same-sex weddings: in law, both parties must be referred to as "wife" if female, or "husband" if both parties are male.

Vows

The wedding vows are seen by most as the high point of the service. This is the point when the couple make heartfelt statements of love, commitment, and support to one another, in the presence of God, of each other, and their friends and family members. Many couples will have fixed views on the wedding vows that they wish to make. Ideally, the two people will share a common preference, but sometimes there are very different expectations. Work carefully with the couple to ensure that appropriate and agreed vows are spoken and accepted.

Unlike the Declaratory and Contracting Words, there is no legal requirement concerning the wording of wedding vows. This allows the couple the freedom to develop words in partnership with each other and with you. Offer support, but encourage them to work together to formulate vows that are meaningful for them.

Marriage Ceremonies

Wedding service at a glance: for a church or meeting house

Traditional vows are still very popular. They might include the following:

> I, FULL NAME, take you, FULL NAME, to be my lawful wedded husband/wife –
> To have and to hold from this day forward
> For better, for worse,
> For richer, for poorer,
> In sickness and in health,
> To love and to cherish,
> Till death us do part,
> According to God's holy law,
> And this is my solemn vow.

Here is one possible alternative:

> I, FULL NAME, take you, FULL NAME, to be my lawful wedded husband/wife –
> To have and to hold from this day forward
> For better, for worse,
> For richer, for poorer,
> In sickness and in health,
> To love and to cherish,
> Till death us do part.
> With my whole heart, and with my complete and earnest devotion,
> I give you my love.

Or

> I, FULL NAME, take you, FULL NAME, to be my lawful wedded husband/wife, and I promise you these things:–
> I will be faithful to you and honest with you;
> I will respect you and trust you;
> I will help you and listen to you;
> I will care for you;
> I will share my life with you in plenty and in want.

Wedding service at a glance: for a church or meeting house

Exchange of rings

It is usual, but not required by law, for rings to be exchanged at this point. Usually the best man will be looking after both rings, but this is not essential. Whoever it is should be asked at this point to bring the rings to the front and place them in your hand.

You might want to explain the significance of the rings to the congregation: how they symbolise the eternal circle of life, and the never-ending continuum of love that has been declared by the couple in their vows. If there is a story behind the rings – made by a friend, or the ring of a lost loved one, for example – suggest to the couple that you might tell it to the congregation.

As each partner is invited to place a ring on the finger of their new wife/husband, they may wish to say some words. These could be similar in style to the vows, or something completely different. Here are some suggestions:

> *REBECCA, I give you this ring to wear as a symbol of my love for you.*
>
> Or
>
> *With this ring I join my life with yours. May it be a symbol of my lasting love, of my commitment to you and to us.*

Pronouncement

Having been through the Declaratory Words, the Contracting Words, the vows, and the exchange of rings, the couple are now legally married. This is the perfect moment to make that announcement. It is traditional to invite the couple to kiss (and perhaps encourage some applause from the congregation).

Wedding service at a glance: for a church or meeting house

Wedding address

The wedding address is an opportunity for you, the service leader, to speak a little about the meaning and purpose of marriage, and to celebrate the commitment of the couple. Recognising that many present might be unaware of the history of the building, or the values of Unitarianism, you might want to ensure that some broader context is included. This is also a necessary time for the couple to step back and sit down for a few minutes. It is likely that they will be tired, both physically and emotionally, by this point.

The address need not take long, but topics to include might be what you know of the couple's first meeting, how their story has developed, and the positive aspects of working with them to create the service. Take the opportunity to remind the couple that marriage is a wonderful thing, but that it is not always easy. Point out that differences and problems are quite normal – we are all human – and encourage them to remember the joy and love of this service whenever strength is called upon.

Bring in traditional and non-traditional quotes if you can. However, unless the couple have indicated otherwise, it is suggested that the address should be light, short, and overwhelmingly positive.

The signing of the Register

With the couple now married, it is important that the Register is signed. This might happen in front of the congregation, or perhaps in a separate room. It is good to have some music played during this part, either live or recorded.

There are important legal requirements concerning the Register, its completion, and how it is witnessed. Consult the relevant materials mentioned on page 25 and ensure that you are complying with the law.

Wedding service at a glance: for a church or meeting house

Hymn

If wanted, this is a good opportunity for a second hymn or song.

Prayer

If wanted, this is a time for one further prayer. Perhaps a prayer for the continued happiness of the couple, for strength in adversity, and the triumph of love to shine through.

Benediction

As the happy couple prepare to leave, this is the chance to call for a blessing on them both and their life together – words of love, of happiness, and of peace together.

Music for departure

See Appendix 2 for notes on the use of live and recorded music in rites-of-passage services.

Top tips for wedding services

Print the order of service on A5 sheets, and place the sheets in an A5, plastic-paged presentation folder. As you will be moving around a lot, an A4 folder may be unnecessarily bulky.

Keep a second copy of the service. Place a second copy in an inside pocket, or in your car if you have one. No-one will be pleased or find it funny if you have lost your only copy. Copy the text to your mobile phone too, if possible, for the same reason.

Meet all those involved. If a rehearsal can be arranged, this is a great opportunity to ensure smooth running on the day, and a chance to meet the best man, ushers, witnesses, etc. The ushers will be crucial on the day.

Agree 'rules' with any photographer on the day. Discuss this with the couple too, and agree whether flash photography is acceptable, and how close you will allow the photographer to get during the service. Camera-lens quality these days means there is rarely a need for very close proximity.

Ensure that the musicians understand their role. Often a couple will ask a friend to play an instrument or lead the singing. Make sure that the singer or musician feels comfortable with the couple's expectations and understands where to stand and what to do.

Choreograph carefully. There is a lot of movement in a wedding, and the couple may be required to sit for readings, stand for vows, etc. Ensure that chairs and sufficient space are available.

Check the readings in advance. Make sure you have read everything that is to be spoken, and that you are comfortable with it.

Speak directly to the couple. Although you are addressing the whole congregation, maintain close and frequent eye contact with the couple throughout the service.

Some alternative wedding services

The following are case studies of services that required some special considerations. They are written by the ministers who prepared and led the services, and they reflect their approach. The case studies do not cover every eventuality, but they do provide suggestions for how you might respond to your own set of circumstances.

Case Study 1: An Interfaith Marriage

It bears repeating that communications are the most important thing to consider and facilitate when a couple are preparing to marry. No matter who they are, the two parties always come to such a union with their own unique vantage points, carrying with them their own unique set of expectations and assumptions, assumptions formed in the melting pot of family dynamics, religious-cultural norms, and individual aspirations.

I recently had the pleasure of conducting a wedding between Claire, a cradle Unitarian, and Amir, a Sunni Muslim. Fundamentally, the same communication principle applies in every case. First of all, I avoid delving immediately into the minutiae of the big day itself: I think it is essential to allow for an exploratory period, during which it is reasonable to expect all parties to familiarise themselves with our Unitarian tradition – not, of course, that they might adopt our religious position, but rather for them to consider if they are happy to be blessed by our community, and whether they are sufficiently in sympathy with our ethos and liberal religious values. In the case of the interfaith couple in question, Amir had no experience of our tradition, but fortunately he could attend a few services, and we were able to chat about various aspects of the movement.

Also during this exploratory period, I give couples a questionnaire to prompt discussion. It is easy to assume that certain fundamental issues have been discussed, when in fact they have not. The questionnaire that I use is wide-ranging, focusing on the couple's relationship, each other's qualities, what prompts them to feel close to one another. It asks about personal preferences, desires, and hopes for the future. I leave open the option to discuss any aspect of the questionnaire with me.

In the case of Claire and Amir, they ended up sharing the whole thing with me, and it ultimately tied into our conversations about the wedding day itself, specifically how each of their backgrounds and religious traditions could be honoured in the course of the service. Broadly speaking, their religious sensibilities were expressed in Amir's wish for family members to be honoured during the service, and Claire's desire for her individual autonomy as an equal party within the marriage to be emphasised. The significance of the coming together of these two families, who on the surface are very different, was a recurring theme during the service. Our chalice-lighting ceremony, for example, involved the mothers of the bride and groom lighting two separate candles, followed by the couple together taking the flame from the two candles to light the chalice, as a symbol of coming together in mutual love and respect.

The readings during the service were drawn from writers whom both partners found inspiring, namely Mahatma Gandhi and Kahlil Gibran. Helping the couple to create a warm and joyful ceremony, having thoroughly discussed all possible aspects and issues in advance, makes for a day that can survive all the inevitable choreographing hiccups, not to mention faulty microphones!

Case Study 2: Another Interfaith Marriage

Jaya and Richard are a young, well educated, professional couple who had been living together for five years before their wedding. At our first interview, Jaya with great sadness told me that she did not think her parents would be attending her wedding. As Hindus, they were unhappy that she was planning to marry someone not of their culture, and that the wedding would be an inter-faith ceremony held in a church. Richard's parents were divorced; he was brought up in a vaguely Christian context, but he himself was more inclined towards Buddhism. Although she did not perceive herself as Hindu, Jaya was anxious for the ceremony to show respect for her parents' religion, in the hope of winning them round before the big day. Jaya was estranged from her brother, but she had an older sister who would accompany her down the aisle. The couple seemed to have an extensive network of supportive friends.

We agreed on an order of service that was an eclectic blend of many elements:

- Background music: Robert Gass
- Lighting of Unitarian chalice
- Processional music: Pachelbel's Canon (recorded)
- Welcome and opening words: about Unitarianism, the sacredness of marriage, and the different elements in the service
- Declaratory Words (legal requirement)
- Reading: Shakespeare's Sonnet 116 (read by Jaya's sister)
- Minister's reflection, including bride's and groom's back stories, their work, shared values, etc, and reading from *The Prophet*: "On Marriage". Followed by silence.
- Reading: "Apache Blessing" (read by Richard's sister)
- Musical interlude: guitar and vocals by a friend of the couple

The ceremony itself proceeded like this:

- Contracting words (legal requirement)
- Lighting of sacred Hindu lamp (Vilakku)
- Exchange of vows (Traditional)
- Exchange of rings (Traditional)

- Giving of the Thali (Golden Thread) by groom to bride – a sign of love and respect
- Blessing of the marriage: The Seven Sacred Steps (around the sacred fire):
  1. May this couple be blessed with an abundance of resources and comforts, and be helpful to one another in all ways.
  2. May this couple be strong and complement one another.
  3. May this couple be blessed with prosperity on all levels.
  4. May this couple be eternally happy.
  5. May this couple be blessed with a happy family life.
  6. May this couple live in perfect harmony, true to their personal values and their joint promises.
  7. May this couple always be the best of friends.
- Signing of the Register (witnessed by best man and Jaya's sister)
- Declaration of Marriage
- Declaration of support by the congregation
- Benediction (Minister): including John O'Donohue's "Blessing for Marriage" from *Benedictus*
- Recessional music: *Better Together* by Jack Johnson

The wedding of Jaya and Richard was certainly the best organised that I've ever been involved in: thanks to the spreadsheet of who was doing what, and when, everyone knew exactly what they were doing. They even managed to find a sunny day sandwiched between two wet blustery days in March. The bride arrived on time, looking absolutely stunning in a traditional white dress with train and veil. And I am glad to report that her parents did attend; they took responsibility for lighting the sacred fire and seemed, in the end, to enjoy the proceedings. Jaya and Richard were delighted with the ceremony, and the guests all loved it. This individual wedding demonstrated the inclusivity and spiritual seriousness that are the hallmarks of Unitarianism.

Case Study 3: A Wedding Blessing Service in a Secular Place (such as a hotel)

This section applies to weddings in England and Wales. The law in Scotland allows wedding services to be conducted in any place, indoors or outdoors.

For many years, it has been possible for couples to choose to marry in buildings other than a church or meeting house. As a result, many couples now choose to get married in an authorised hotel, where accommodation and meals can be arranged in the same place.

As part of the legislation supporting this approach, it is not possible for a legal religious marriage ceremony to be performed in a secular environment, and the legal aspects of such a ceremony are therefore conducted by a local Registrar. This includes the legally required Contracting Words, as well as the signing of the Register. At no point in such a ceremony might there be words of a religious nature, including prayer.

Nevertheless, many couples, while deliberately choosing a secular venue for convenience or aesthetic reasons, will wish to have a religious element in their day; for example, for many, the opportunity to make a commitment before God is essential. It is the case therefore that separate blessing ceremonies – often conducted immediately after the legal secular marriage ceremony – are held to allow this aspect of the couple's wishes to be fulfilled. It is best to conduct this religious service after the legal service, to ensure that there is no suggestion that the blessing service is a legal marriage service (which would not be allowed); if the couple are already married, this of course cannot be an issue. If the religious blessing is to take place after the legal ceremony, it is good practice to discuss the plans with the Registrar, to avoid any possible confusion.

The blessing service can include all the aspects of a usual wedding, although Contracting Words and the Signing of the Register are not required. The couple may, however, wish to wait for this service to declare their vows to one another.

Alternatively, the blessing service might be a much shorter ceremony, with prayer, vows, and perhaps a hymn. The elements detailed in the first part of this chapter might be used in this service too.

3 Funerals

Introduction

The only certainty in life is that we will eventually die. However, discussion of our own demise, or the death of close relatives and friends, remains, for many, a taboo topic. But if the topic is not discussed, the lack of planning will leave the bereaved uncertain of the funeral wishes of the deceased, alongside pressing issues such as the division of any estate.

The structure and content of a funeral service can take many forms. In some religious traditions, the focus of the funeral, led by an ordained or otherwise appropriate celebrant, is the hoped-for transition of an individual's soul from this life to another life beyond death. Others will focus entirely on the needs of the congregation – those close relatives and friends left bereft and upset by the death – with a service designed to meet their needs at an often difficult time.

Religious funeral ceremonies vary according to geographical location, beliefs, requirements, scripture, local tradition, and so on. For Unitarians, there is usually no specific theological or religious requirement for a ceremony to guide the soul of the deceased to a life after death. Where there is a belief that such an afterlife exists, it would be unusual for anyone to expect that the intercession of a minister or otherwise authorised person would be necessary to ensure safe passage of the soul. For those, perhaps the majority, who do not believe in an afterlife, the funeral service is a time for the mourners to pay formal tribute to the deceased one final time, and to gather in community to share stories and support one another. For Unitarians, therefore, funerals are primarily a time to remember, reflect, and give thanks for a life lived and now ended.

Unitarian funerals can be held at a church or crematorium, or simply at a graveside. There is no theological requirement for a funeral to be held within a certain number of days after death, nor for a specific rite to be read. The timing and structure of the service can therefore take any form, although this will be constrained in part by the surroundings and the amount of time allocated by the church or crematorium.

The unique nature of a good Unitarian funeral comes from careful and considered discussion and engagement with the next of kin and those closest to the deceased. A funeral usually provides a once-only opportunity to say a formal farewell and pay tribute to a loved one, and for the service leader the funeral is one of the most challenging yet also rewarding services that can be led. To be with someone at their most raw, and to help them through an often paralysing time of mourning, is a privilege as well as a responsibility.

There are no legal requirements concerning funeral ceremonies. Such rites are entirely discretionary and separate from the necessary registration of the death and formal disposal of the body (which funeral directors and crematorium or cemetery staff are better qualified to deal with).

Options for the nature and structure of funerals and memorial services include a single service at the crematorium; a service at the crematorium followed by a memorial service – the same day or later – at a separate place, often a church; a church service followed by a burial; a church service followed by a service at the crematorium; and a church service followed by the removal of the deceased to the crematorium, without a second service. This list is not exhaustive, but it covers the main options.

This chapter contains suggested Orders of Service for Funerals held in churches, crematoria, or cemeteries. There is a separate section on the use of music. There are also short case studies, written by different ministers, on specific adaptations that they needed to make in order to reflect special circumstances. The chapter concludes with a list of 'Top Tips' – essential practical advice on conducting a better service.

Preparation

A funeral service is a tender and sensitive rite of passage. In a Unitarian context, it is held to comfort those who knew the deceased well – family, friends, colleagues – and to recognise and celebrate the truth and love within the life of the person who has died.

If you knew the deceased personally, as a member of your congregation or in another way, it is especially important to give careful consideration to the purpose of the service, and the emotions that it is likely to arouse. Think very carefully before agreeing to lead a service if the deceased person was a close relative or friend of yours. It is the role of the celebrant to lead the service and guide others through it, so although there is great value in empathy, you need to assess realistically whether you will be able to hold your own emotions in check. If you can't, it may be better to help the family to find an alternative leader for the service.

Essential to a meaningful service is working closely with the family, or nearest friends, to ensure that their needs and their wishes are met. The advantage of Unitarian rites of passage is the freedom to flex and fix a service in whatever way is required: there are no set words – no liturgy – so you and the family are free to create something personal. A face-to-face planning meeting is best, but if that is not possible, then email and phone contact should be frequent.

When you meet, be aware that the family are likely to be in a state of emotional shock. Ensure that you are ready for that, and mentally prepare for it. Don't ask, for example, "How are you today?" in a bright, jaunty voice; it is all too easy to slip into this automatic response mode (we can all do it).

Your meetings with the family are an opportunity to talk through options for the service, to help them understand that it is an opportunity for both celebration and remembrance. Use the 'Service at a Glance' (below) to guide your questions as you create the service together.

Music can be very important at funeral services, often chosen to inspire memories of specific occasions or events in the life of the deceased and, sometimes, their bereaved partner or family. Take care to work with the family on this element, making suggestions but being open to the fact that the favoured music may not 'fit' ; you may need to work creatively and sensitively to balance the wishes of the family against the potential for inappropriate tempo or tunes.

Funeral service at a glance: at a crematorium

A crematorium service is becoming more usual for funerals, and it will often take the place of a funeral at a church or meeting house. An advantage of this is that there are likely to be a number of professionals present to support and guide you and the family through the service. However, it is important to note that crematorium services are generally strictly controlled in terms of timing, and the slot that you have been allocated cannot be extended or allowed to overrun. This requires an additional level of control, and a willingness to intervene to ensure that any contributions from the family and/or friends are controlled. Taking this into account, the service at the crematorium can be just as creative and personal as a church service, or anywhere with less restrictive time limits, and it is the role of the minister or celebrant to ensure that the needs of the mourners are met.

Traditionally, the minister, or service leader, will be present at the roadside when the hearse, carrying the coffin, arrives at the crematorium. It is usual for the funeral directors to be present too, ensuring that people are taking their seats and/or waiting for the coffin as necessary. If the close family are already present, use this time to talk to them, reassure them that shows of emotion are fine, and that this is their opportunity to pay public tribute to their loved one. If anyone is doing a reading as part of the service, use this time too to ensure that they are composed and comfortable – and assure them that you are ready to step in and read if they need you to.

Once the hearse has arrived, and the undertakers are ready to remove the coffin to the chapel, compose yourself and watch it closely. From this point, you are the person positioned closest to the coffin, and you will lead the service from here. When the funeral director has indicated that he or she is ready, begin to walk steadily and with purpose into the chapel. You are leading the dead to the space of remembrance. This

---
Funeral service at a glance: at a crematorium
---

is a solemn and privileged responsibility. Lead the coffin to the front, and then step towards your reading desk while the undertakers put the coffin at rest. Then the undertakers will usually bow to the coffin and leave the chapel.

There will often be music playing at this point – either by an organist or other musician, or on a CD controlled from elsewhere. The exit of the undertakers is usually the cue for the music to end too. Wait until the undertakers have left, and the music has stopped, before you start speaking.

Opening words

No matter how formal or informal the service will be, this is a solemn and important moment. The opening words will set the tone of the service, but also mark the formal start of proceedings. A quotation is often a good way to mark the transition from preparation to delivery. This adaptation of words from Homer might be suitable:

> *The Sun rises and the Sun goes down. The wind turns and turns again. All streams run into the seas. Yet the sea is never filled.*
> *As is the life of the leaves, so is that of men and women. The wind scatters the leaves to the ground; the vigorous forest puts forth others, and they grow in the spring season. Soon one generation comes and another ceases.*

Words of welcome and introduction

An opportunity to welcome the family and friends to the crematorium. A time to explain the purpose of the ceremony (one of farewell, reflection, and, if appropriate, a celebration of a life well lived), to explain the order in which things will happen, and reassure everyone that they will be helped with all words and actions throughout.

Funeral service at a glance: at a crematorium

Chalice lighting and stillness

For services such as this, people may have travelled long distances, and there is a need for a disparate and unrelated group of people to reflect on what has brought them all together at this time. If the service is taking place in a church, this might be a good time to light a chalice or candle and bring everyone to a point of stillness and quiet for a minute or two. If it is in a crematorium, lighting a candle will probably not be possible, so you need to create silence and stillness without one. Some suitable words might be the following:

> *We are gathered to remember, and to celebrate a life. We have travelled from many places to be here today. We have worried about the journey, about timings, about parking or taxis. Put those thoughts to one side. We are here, gathered in love for SAM.*
>
> *Let us take a short time in stillness and silence to calm our minds and our bodies. To bring ourselves fully into this place.*

Prayer

The silence might be broken by reflective words or words of prayer, calling on God, or the Spirit of Love, to be present at the ceremony – in our hearts, and all around. How this is phrased should be determined through your conversations with the family in preparation for the service: gauge the level of traditional language required, and create a service with that in mind.

Some family members may ask for, or expect, the Lord's Prayer at this point. It is a prayer that many others present might also know, so it can be inclusive. It may, however, make those who are not from a Christian background feel excluded. Make these points clear when working with the family on the service, and let their considerations guide the

Funerals

Funeral service at a glance: at a crematorium

---

decision on whether to include it. Bear in mind the religious affiliation (or otherwise) of the deceased, if known, to help determine whether he or she would have found the Lord's Prayer appropriate or not.

Hymn or song

A hymn or song provides a good opportunity for the gathering to join together as one. If many of the group are not regular church-goers, they may find traditional hymns quite hard to follow and sing – although traditional funeral hymns such as 'Be Thou My Vision' and 'The Lord's My Shepherd' are popular and appropriate.

Alternatively, it is increasingly common for people to choose songs that were favourites of the deceased, or songs that evoke memories of specific events in their lives. This might be a time to play a recording of one of those. If there are several tracks to be played during the service, one of the slower-paced ones may be helpful here.

Reading(s)

Readings may be traditional, perhaps from the Bible, or they may be more modern poems or stories. Listed in Annex C to this book are several suggestions of appropriate readings and poems; the Further Resources section contains further suggestions. However, this is a good opportunity to acknowledge the particular interests of the deceased: if, for example, they were a reader of J R R Tolkien, then appropriate readings might be found from his works.

The internet gives access to a wealth of appropriate material. However, much of its content might contain one or two words or phrases that make it entirely inappropriate. Ensure that you have read through all the readings before the service, and suggested edits or alternatives where necessary.

Funeral service at a glance: at a crematorium

Help the family to decide who might be best to read these one, two, or three passages. It might be appropriate for a sibling, daughter/son, or good friend to do a reading. But bear in mind that they may not, at the last moment, feel able to read without bursting into tears. Reassure all readers that they can drop out at any point – there is no shame in this – and you will stand ready to read in their place.

Eulogy

The eulogy is an opportunity for someone – sometimes you, sometimes a close relative or friend – to tell the life story of the deceased. Use your meetings with the family to gather the full story, with as much information as possible, and, if you are writing the eulogy, try to draw themes from the information, telling the story of a unique and special person. For style, you will need to consider the family's wishes, but also read sample obituaries in the broadsheet newspapers to form a sense of appropriate themes and level of detail. The eulogy is, however, more than an obituary. You should, where possible, include the names of those present when they appear in the story, and look at them when you refer to them. Or gesture towards them, if that feels right. People like to be acknowledged as part of the story.

The length of the eulogy will be determined by the time available. It usually lasts up to five minutes – but check this.

As with the readings, reassure anyone reading the eulogy – or part of it – that they can drop out at any point, and you will stand ready to read in their place.

Funeral service at a glance: at a crematorium

Stillness, reflection, and music

After the eulogy, the congregation will most likely have memories, stories, and images of the deceased swirling around in their minds. This is the ideal time to bring silence to the proceedings once more, allowing those memories to be savoured. Moving from the silence into music – again perhaps a favoured piece from the deceased's collection – will help people to grieve, even to cry. You might want to use words such as these:

> *All of us here will recognise SAMIRA from the stories we have heard.*
>
> *With a huge love and devotion for her family, she sought connection. Connection to people and things that she cared about.*
>
> *Now, following the memories that we've shared, I invite you to spend a few moments in stillness and quiet, connecting, dwelling close with SAMIRA, with Mum, with Nana, and allowing your own distinctive memory of her to become clear in your mind's eye – your stories engraved on your heart.*
>
> *We shall share a quiet time, and then some time where music will allow us to reflect further.*
>
> *Let us sit quietly and remember SAMIRA.*
>
> *[One minute's silence]*
>
> *MUSIC*

Funeral service at a glance: at a crematorium

The Committal

The Committal is the part of the service where, traditionally, the soul of the deceased is commended to the keeping of the Eternal, and the body committed to the earth. For many families and individuals this committal is instead a commitment to memory, to the greater legacy of the world and all the people in it and before us. Your words must reflect the nature of the service and the wishes of the family – the religious, humanist, or atheist wishes of those present, and recognise the worth of all.

If the service is being held in a crematorium, this is normally the moment when the coffin is removed from view – usually by the closing of a curtain. This is a very emotionally charged moment, a tender moment, when the final farewell is given.

Words such as the following might be used. These words would be appropriate for an older person who had lived a good and long life. Ensure that the words you choose reflect the life story and departure of the deceased.

> *We have shared many beautiful memories and stories this afternoon.*
>
> *We are saddened by the loss of SAMIRA – we will not see her again. Yet we might be strengthened and encouraged in the knowledge that her life was lived so well – that she brought such pleasure, love, fun, and joy to the world, and that legacy remains with each of us.*
>
> *Now, please stand for the Committal.*
>
> *To everything there is a season,*
> *and a time to every purpose under the heavens:*
> *a time to be born, and a time to die.*
>
> *Death has come in due season for SAMIRA.*

Funeral service at a glance: at a crematorium

Her hopes and dreams we commit into our minds and our wills.
Her loves we commit into our hearts.
Her spirit we commit into the keeping of the Eternal.

Earth to earth, ashes to ashes, dust to dust.

We now commit SAMIRA's body to be returned into the elements from which it came.

We pray for safe onward passage of her soul.

May peace be upon her.

At this point you will normally press a button to bring a curtain around the coffin. This is a highly emotional moment, and you need to ensure that people are ready and can cope with this. Talk with the family before the service, to agree how the curtain will be managed. While most will either assume or request that the curtain is drawn, some will ask that the coffin is left in view at this time – often suggesting that they will wish the coffin to remain visible even as the congregation leaves at the end. This needs to be discussed very carefully during the preparations. In my experience, it is better for all that the coffin is in some way removed at this point, usually by drawing a curtain – although some crematoria still have a 'lowering' function – because a visible coffin from this point is likely to add to the stress of loss.

It is worth emphasising to all the gathered mourners that it is perfectly reasonable to cry at this point. Funerals are an opportunity to express deeply felt emotion.

Prayer

If wanted, this is a time for one further prayer: perhaps a prayer for life to be hallowed by memories of the deceased, and to seek peace for the close family and friends left behind. This is a time for prayer for the future, recognising that the committal is complete.

Benediction

Some words to provide strength and love in the coming days and weeks as the congregation leaves the building. Words such as:

> *We are thankful for this time of sharing and for all the special memories that you have brought with you.*
>
> *May the love and friendship that we have shared today go now into our daily lives: giving comfort in our sorrows, delight in all the joys to come, drawing life and vitality from our very being.*
>
> *May peace be with us and among us all, now and for evermore.*
>
> *Amen*

Music for departure

This is a suitable opportunity for some final music, reflecting the life of the deceased. It is often the moment to play something faster paced or upbeat, reflecting the commitment to continue life anew.

After a minute or so of this music, the funeral director will normally ask the congregation to leave the building, one row at a time. They will start with members of the close family, and indicate when people are to leave. When you see this begin to happen, you need to leave the building and wait just outside the door by which people will leave. Be ready to shake hands with everyone. Some may not wish to, but many will.

When all have left the building, walk at the back of the line towards the exit point.

Funeral service at a glance: for a church (leading to burial outside)

It is more traditional to hold a funeral service at a church or meeting house than a crematorium, but the number of church funerals is declining. Often a funeral will be held in a church only if the deceased was a regular or occasional attender there, although this is not always the case.

Preparation is very similar to that for a crematorium service, although it is likely that you will not be bound by time constraints in the same way. This can enable a more creative approach. Much of what follows is based on the approach outlined for a crematorium, but there are changes towards the end.

Traditionally, the minister, or service leader, will be present at the roadside when the hearse, carrying the coffin, arrives at the church. It is usual for the funeral directors to be present too, ensuring that people are taking their seats and/or waiting for the coffin, as appropriate. If the close family are already at the church, use this time to talk to them, reassure them that shows of emotion are fine, and that this is their opportunity to pay public tribute to their loved one. If anyone is doing a reading as part of the service, use this time too to ensure that they are composed and comfortable – and assure them that you are ready to step in and read if they need you to.

Once the car has arrived, and the undertakers are ready to remove the coffin to the church, compose yourself and watch it closely. When the funeral director has indicated that he or she is ready, begin to walk steadily and with purpose ahead of the coffin. You are leading the dead to the space of remembrance. This is a solemn and privileged responsibility. Lead the coffin to the front, and then step towards your reading desk while the undertakers put the coffin at rest. Then they will usually bow to the coffin and leave the church.

Funeral service at a glance: for a church (leading to burial outside)

There will often be music playing at this point – played either by an organist or other musician, or on a CD controlled from elsewhere. If this is your church, you will need to have ensured that there is someone to be responsible for the music throughout the service. The exit of the undertakers is usually the cue for the music to end too. Wait until the undertakers have left, and the music has stopped, before you start speaking.

Opening words

No matter how formal or informal the service will be, this is a solemn and important moment. The opening words will set the tone of the service, but also mark the formal start to proceedings. A quotation is often a good way to mark the transition from preparation to delivery. This adaptation of words from Homer might be suitable:

> *The Sun rises and the Sun goes down. The wind turns and turns again.*
> *All streams run into the seas. Yet the sea is never filled.*
> *As is the life of the leaves, so is that of men and women. The wind scatters the leaves to the ground; the vigorous forest puts forth others, and they grow in the spring season. Soon one generation comes, and another ceases.*

Words of welcome and introduction

An opportunity to welcome the family and friends to the church. A time to explain the purpose of the ceremony (one of farewell, reflection, and, if appropriate, a celebration of a life well lived), set out the order in which things will happen, and reassure everyone that they will be helped with all words and actions throughout.

Funeral service at a glance: for a church (leading to burial outside)

Chalice lighting and stillness

For services such as this, people may have travelled long distances, and there is a need for a potentially disparate and unrelated group of people to reflect on what has brought them together at this time.

In a church, this might be a good time to light a chalice or candle and bring everyone to a point of stillness and quiet for a minute or two. These words might be suitable:

We are gathered to remember, and to celebrate a life. We have travelled from many places to be here today. We have worried about the journey, about timings, about parking or taxis. Put those thoughts to one side. We are here, gathered in love for SAM.

Let us take a short time in stillness and silence to calm our minds and our bodies. To bring ourselves fully into this place.

Prayer

The silence might be broken by reflective words or words of prayer, calling on God, or the Spirit of Love, to be present at the ceremony – in our hearts, and all around. How this is phrased should be determined through your conversations with the family in preparation for the service: gauge the level of traditional language required, and create a service with that in mind.

Some family members may ask for, or expect, the Lord's Prayer at this point. It is a prayer that many others present might also know, so its use can be inclusive. But it might make those who are not from a Christian background feel excluded. Make these points clear when working with the family on the service, and let their considerations guide the decision on whether to include it. Bear in mind the religious affiliation (or otherwise) of the deceased, if known, to help

---
Funeral service at a glance: for a church (leading to burial outside)
---

determine whether he or she would have found the Lord's Prayer appropriate or not.

Hymn or song

A hymn or song provides a good opportunity for the mourners to join together as one. If many of the group are not regular church-goers, they may find traditional hymns quite hard to follow and sing – although traditional funeral hymns such as 'Be Thou My Vision' and 'The Lord's My Shepherd' are popular and appropriate.

Alternatively, it is increasingly common for people to choose songs that were favourites of the deceased, or songs that evoke memories of specific events in their lives. This might be a time to play a recording of one of those. If there are several tracks to be played during the service, one of the slower-paced ones may be helpful here.

Reading(s)

Readings may be traditional, perhaps taken from the Bible, or they may be poems or stories of more modern origin. Annex C to this book offers some suggestions, and the Further Resources section lists a number of books containing appropriate readings and poems. However, this is a good opportunity to take account of the interests of the deceased: if, for example, he or she has been a reader of J R R Tolkien, then appropriate readings might be found from his works.

The internet gives access to a wealth of appropriate material. However, much of its content might contain one or two words or phrases that make the text entirely inappropriate. Ensure that you have read through all the readings before the service and have suggested edits or alternatives where necessary.

Funeral service at a glance: for a church (leading to burial outside)

Help the family to decide who might be best to read these one, two, or three passages. It might be appropriate for a sibling, daughter/son, or good friend to do readings. But bear in mind that they may not, at the last moment, feel able to read without bursting into tears. Reassure all readers that they can drop out at any point – there is no shame in this – and you will stand ready to read in their place.

Eulogy

The eulogy is the point in the service where someone – sometimes you, sometimes a close relative or friend – will tell the life story of the deceased. Use your meetings with the family to gather as much information as possible, to compile the full story, and, if you are writing the eulogy, try to draw themes from the information, telling the story of a unique and special person. For style, you will need to consider the family's wishes, but also read obituaries in the broadsheet newspapers to form a sense of appropriate themes and levels of detail. The eulogy is, however, more than an obituary. You should, where possible, give the names of those present when they appear in the story, and look at them when you say their names. Or gesture towards them, if that feels right. People like to be acknowledged as part of the story.

The length of the eulogy will be determined by the time available. It usually lasts about five minutes. The advantage of a church-based service is often that you are able to be more flexible with timings, allowing for a longer eulogy, or additional reflections from family and friends of the deceased.

As with the readings, reassure anyone reading the eulogy – or part of it – that they can drop out at any point and you will stand ready to read in their place.

Funeral service at a glance: for a church (leading to burial outside)

Stillness, reflection, and music

After the eulogy, the congregation will most likely have memories, stories, and images of the deceased swirling around in their minds. This is the ideal time to bring silence into the proceedings once more, allowing those memories to be savoured. Then moving from silence into music – again perhaps a favoured piece from the deceased's collection – will help people to grieve. You might want to use words such as these:

> All of us here will recognise ALICE from the stories we have heard.
>
> With a huge love and devotion for her family, ALICE sought connection. Connection to people and things that she cared about.
>
> Now, following the memories we've shared, I invite you to spend a few moments in stillness and quiet, connecting, dwelling close with ALICE – with Mum, with Nana – and allowing your own distinctive memory of her to become clear in your mind's eye – your stories engraved on your heart.
>
> We shall share a quiet time, and then some time when music will allow us to reflect further.
>
> Let us sit quietly and remember ALICE.
>
> [One Minute of Silence]
>
> MUSIC

Funeral service at a glance: for a church (leading to burial outside)

Moving outside

At this point, it is good to move the service outside the church, to process to the place of burial. If this is in the churchyard, the procedure will be quite simple. However, if the burial ground is a drive away, you need to prepare the congregation for this too. The following words might be suitable:

> *We have shared many beautiful and wonderful memories and stories this afternoon.*
>
> *We are saddened by the loss of ALICE – we will not see her again. Yet we might be strengthened and encouraged in the knowledge that her life was lived so well – that she brought such pleasure, love, fun, and joy to the world, and that legacy will remain with each of us from this day forward.*
>
> *We will leave this place now and, following ALICE, will move to the churchyard for the burial and a chance to say goodbye.*
>
> *Please stand and wait to be asked to follow the coffin.*

At this point, the coffin-bearers (usually the funeral directors) will arrange to carry the coffin outside. You should lead the coffin, and the congregation will be led out, close family members first, to follow the coffin. You will need to agree this with the funeral directors before the service.

Once everyone is gathered at the graveside, the Committal can take place.

Funeral service at a glance: for a church (leading to burial outside)

The Committal

The Committal is the part of the service where, traditionally, the soul of the deceased is commended to the keeping of the Eternal, and the body committed to the earth. For many families and individuals, this committal is instead a commitment to memory, to the greater legacy of the world and all the people in it, and those who went before us. Your words must reflect the nature of the service and the wishes of the family – respecting the religious, humanist, or atheist wishes of those present, and recognising the worth of all.

This is a very emotionally charged moment, a tender moment, when the final farewell is given. Words such as the following might be used. These words would be appropriate for an older person who had lived a good and long life. Ensure that the words you choose reflect the life story and departure of the deceased.

> *To everything there is a season,*
>
> *and a time to every purpose under the heavens:*
>
> *a time to be born, and a time to die.*
>
> *Death has come in due season for ALICE.*
>
> *Her hopes and dreams we commit into our minds and our wills.*
>
> *Her loves we commit into our hearts.*
>
> *Her spirit we commit into the keeping of the Eternal.*
>
> *Earth to earth, ashes to ashes, dust to dust.*
>
> *We now commit ALICE's body to be returned to the elements from which it came.*
>
> *We pray for safe onward passage of her soul.*
>
> *May peace be upon her.*

Funeral service at a glance: for a church (leading to burial outside)

At this point, the coffin will be lowered slowly into the grave, and, if agreed with the family and funeral directors beforehand, you and then others may wish to scatter earth on the coffin, in a final farewell. If this is desired, you should let the gathered people know this, and invite all those present to do likewise.

Prayer

Once the scattering of earth is complete, there is time for one further prayer. Perhaps a prayer for life to be lived in faithful memory of the deceased, and to seek peace for the close family and friends left behind. This is a time for prayer for the future, recognising that the Committal is complete.

Benediction

Some words to provide strength and love in the coming days and weeks as the congregation departs. Words such as these:

We are thankful for this time of sharing and for all the special memories you have brought with you.

May the love and friendship that we have shared today go now into our daily lives: giving comfort in sorrow, and delight in all the joys to come, drawing life and vitality from our differences and our very being.

May peace be with us and among us all, now and for evermore.

Amen

Funeral service at a glance: for a church (leading to burial outside)

Departure

Having finished the service, you should go to the family and offer final condolences. Shake hands and then move slowly away from the group. Usually, the family and friends will wait awhile at the graveside, remembering and talking among themselves. It is usually best to remain at a discreet distance, but within sight, and allow the group to break up and disperse naturally. Some may wish to come over and thank you; others will not.

A funeral in a church, followed by transit to a crematorium

You may occasionally be asked to conduct a funeral service at a church or meeting house, followed by the transit of the coffin to a crematorium for a short service of Committal. The structure is very similar to that presented above for a church service followed by burial, with adjustments to the wording as necessary.

The Committal element may be brief – following the form of the burial, above – or it may be a more full crematorium service. Work with the family to ensure that they are aware of the added emotion generated by two full services, should that be their initial intent.

Sevice at a glance:
for an interment of ashes

Occasionally, you may be asked to lead a service of Interment (burial) of Ashes. This will often be a continuation of a service that you have previously led, with the family now ready to say a final farewell. Preparation for this service is just as important as for the previous full ceremony. For the family or friends, the mere presence or thought of the ashes will bring old memories to the surface, and prompt a deep emotional response.

Ensure that a suitably sized hole is already prepared in the churchyard for the interment – and be prepared for the surprising volume of ashes that will be buried.

The family will usually bring the ashes with them. If the service is to be held in the church or meeting house, either take the ashes yourself to the table at the front, or ask the family to do so. If the service is being held in the churchyard itself, agree beforehand whether you will have placed the ashes alongside the hole in advance, or whether perhaps they will be held by the family throughout.

Words of welcome and introduction

This is the opportunity to welcome the family and friends to the churchyard. If you previously led the funeral service, make reference to that. Set out what the service will consist of, and explain what will happen. Here are some sample words:

> *Earlier this year we were sad to learn of the passing of ADAM JONES, husband, father, grandfather, member of the congregation at this chapel, and friend to so many.*

Sevice at a glance: for an interment of ashes

> *Now, we gather in this place, where ADAM was so committed and giving, each to say a final goodbye to ADAM, and to commit his ashes to the earth of this churchyard alongside those of his wife, MARY.*
>
> *In this place of peace, we will hear a reading, we will listen to music, and we will say prayers. It will be a short and simple service.*
>
> *Importantly, there will be a period of stillness and reflection during the ceremony when all will be able to remember Adam in peace, and together in community.*

Prayer

An opportunity for prayer and reflection. This is the chance for people to come together, perhaps with an agreed prayer for all to speak – the Lord's Prayer might be a popular choice, but offer alternatives too, such as this:

> *Universal Spirit, God of many names,*
>
> *We lift our hearts in search of the inward strength we need to face life's varied experiences of joy and of sorrow.*
>
> *At times like this, when one to whom we have been joined by ties of kinship and love has been taken from us, we seek the peace of acceptance.*

Stillness

Let the congregation know that there will be a period of stillness now, to make a final connection with the earthly body of the deceased. Gently bring the gathered community to a place of stillness and calm.

Sevice at a glance: for an interment of ashes

If still inside the meeting house or church, you might wish to close this time of reflection with a piece of music. Sometimes it can be helpful to choose the same music as that played at the Committal. Work through this with the family as you prepare.

Leaving the building

If appropriate, this is the time for the congregation to leave the building and move to the churchyard. Agree with the family beforehand whether you or they will carry the ashes. Either is appropriate. Either way, it is right that you lead the gathering to the final resting place outside.

Reading

At the final resting place, I recommend that the ashes are placed next to the hole in the ground. Gather the close family and friends around, and read some final words. Words from the Biblical book of Ecclesiastes would be appropriate, but other forms of words can be equally profound.

> *To everything there is a season,*
> *And a time to every purpose under the heaven:*
> *A time to be born, and a time to die;*
> *A time to plant, and a time to pluck up that which is planted;*
> *A time to kill, and a time to heal;*
> *A time to break down, and a time to build up;*
> *A time to weep, and a time to laugh;*
> *A time to mourn, and a time to dance;*
> *A time to cast away stones, and a time to gather stones together;*
> *A time to embrace, and a time to refrain from embracing;*
> *A time to seek, and a time to lose;*
> *A time to keep, and a time to throw away;*

Sevice at a glance: for an interment of ashes

A time to tear, and a time to sew;
A time to keep silence, and a time to speak;
A time to love, and a time for peace.

Placing the ashes in the ground

Placement of the ashes in the ground needs to be handled carefully and sensitively. You may be surprised at the volume of ashes, and, as mentioned in the introduction to this section, you will want to be sure beforehand that the hole is properly prepared and of a suitable size. I recommend having a perfectly clean trowel at hand for this part of the service. Use words such as these:

Out of the ground we are taken,
and to dust we shall all return.

Earth to Earth,
Ashes to Ashes,
Dust to Dust.

Then, placing a small amount of ashes on the trowel, invite a member of the family to deposit them in the ground. Follow this with offers to others present. When all who wish to do so have taken part, you will want to add a small amount yourself.

You need to agree with the family beforehand whether all the remaining ashes are then placed in the ground, or whether you leave the remainder at the side, for the deposition to be completed after the family has left the area. The sheer amount of ash can be distressing when seen being poured into the hole, so you need to guide the mourners gently.

Sevice at a glance: for an interment of ashes

Final words

Some final words, a prayer and benediction, will bring closure to the service. Here are some suggested words:

We have committed the ashes of RASHEED to the keeping of the Earth which bears us all. We are glad that RASHEED lived, that we knew his friendship, and walked with him on the path of life.

The memory of him and his character is deeply cherished.

In love we remember him.

And in thinking of RASHEED in this manner, let us go now in quietness of spirit and live in peace, in loving friendship, one with another.

Amen

Top tips for funeral services

Print the text of the service on A5 sheets, and place them in an A5, plastic-paged presentation folder. You will be moving around a lot, and will find that A4 can be unnecessarily bulky. Also, the desk at the crematorium may be too small for A4.

Keep a second copy of the service. Place a second copy of the whole text in an inside pocket, or in your car if you drive to the service. You never know when you may need a back-up. No-one will be pleased or find it funny if you've lost the text – and crematorium timekeeping means that you cannot go back to fetch a new copy from your office. Copy it to your mobile phone too, if possible, for the same reason.

Check the readings and eulogy in advance. All manner of well-meant or overlooked comments can be inappropriate. Make sure you've read everything that is to be spoken, and that you are comfortable with it. You may need to read things that others intended to read, but find themselves incapable of reading.

Speak directly to the family. Although you are addressing the whole congregation, maintain close and frequent eye contact with the family and close friends. Allow them to assume that you are talking only to them.

Get to know the family before the service. They will look to you as a friend and guide.

Some alternative funeral services

The following are case studies of services that required some special considerations. They are written by the ministers who prepared and led the services, and they reflect their approach. The case studies do not cover every eventuality, but they do provide ideas for how you might respond to your own set of circumstances.

Case Study 1: A Service for a Still-born Child

One of the hardest funerals I have ever conducted was for a full-term, still-born infant. Aside from the obvious grief, the situation was worsened by the fact that the parents' marriage was breaking down. Perhaps they hoped that a baby would help to salvage their ailing relationship – but it was not to be. Usually after the loss of a baby, parents at least have each other for mutual support, and there is the hope, if unspoken, that they can try to conceive another child. This couple, while momentarily united in grief at the loss of their only child, were contending with the likely reality that they had no future together.

Both were present at the funeral planning meeting, each bringing family members for support. They tried to 'be there' for each other – but the atmosphere was tense. I wanted to honour the wishes of both parents in planning the ceremony, although my instinct was to focus on the needs of the mother, who had been struck a double blow by the loss of her baby and her husband's absence before and during pregnancy.

I tried to allay any feelings of guilt and recrimination; particularly the mother's concern that the stress and strain of relationship problems might have contributed to the still-birth. As for the father – whatever he had done, or not done, he too was grieving. I was not there to play judge and jury, or act as a marriage counsellor, but to ensure that this act of remembrance was as healing as possible for them both.

I affirmed the love that they had for their baby, especially the mother; she *was* a mother – and would *always* be a mother; she had carried and cherished a child in her body for nine months, and felt life move within her – and such memories could never be taken away.

The funeral directors were attentive and helpful. Both they and I waived our fee (as I believe is the norm in the case of infant death). We held a service at the church; the little coffin was carried in by both parents, laid on a table covered with the cloth that their baby had been wrapped in at birth. Only the parents and a few family members were present. I normalised their tears; theirs was as big a loss as any other – if not more so, because they had so few precious memories to hold on to.

They lit candles and voiced their sorrow; they played recordings of the lullabies that their child had heard in the womb. There was a printed order of service (just as there would be with any other funeral, validating the gravity of their loss). On the front was a tiny footprint taken from their child – a poignant and visible reminder of a precious life, too soon cut short.

The service was followed by a short committal at the crematorium. The parents had no strong faith to fall back on. There could be no promise of a bright hereafter. This lack of religious framework made it harder for me; I found myself *wanting* to offer the comfort afforded by traditional sentiments. But I honoured their wishes for a broadly humanist funeral, while calling on the consolation of poetry and the imagination with a few lines from Emily Dickinson, who envisaged heaven as a vast blue sky in June. Flowers were laid on the little coffin as the mourners said their final goodbyes.

Feedback suggests that it was a good enough ceremony. I hope it helped the parents to feel affirmed; to know that the brief life of their child *mattered* – that their emotions were as valid as those of any other grieving parent – and that they were not to blame for their infant's death. I gave the mother a print-out of my words afterwards, to add to the few tangible objects that would serve as precious mementos of her child's brief existence.

This was not a time for glib answers. Some might think "Maybe it was for the best, given that the marriage was over... the mother might have struggled on her own... the child would be an unhappy reminder of a broken relationship". But it is not our role as ministers to rationalise, or offer false comfort; rather we are called to bear witness to grief in all its rawness – and, at the same time, to hold out hope for the future – albeit a future, in this case, in which the parents would go their separate ways and move on with their individual lives.

It seems imperative that still-births are fully recognised – that the baby is named, that photographs are taken, and a full funeral ceremony provided, should the parents want this. Thankfully this is increasingly recognised by medics, clerics, and funeral directors, and more resources and support are now available for parents of still-born infants, thanks particularly to the work of SANDS, the stillbirth and neonatal death charity.

Some words for the funeral of a still-born infant

"This is an especially sad day, because grief for the loss of a child is hardest of all to bear. As Thomas Lynch says, '... *burying infants, we bury the future*...'. And this grief is particularly sharp when the child is still-born – as summed up in a poem by Elizabeth Jennings: *'For a Child Born Dead'*.

"Today is a time to acknowledge the depths of grief – to name your sadness. The grief you feel is the measure of your love – for only the unloved go un-mourned. But today, alongside the grief, we acknowledge the gladness that X brought, if only for a brief time. For a short while, you knew your baby – as only a mother can ... X would have been aware of you from within the womb – familiar with the sound of your voice, your routine of sleeping and waking, hearing the music you played, the lullabies you sang....

"There will never be anyone in the world to replace X. S/he was your child; and will always be so. There will be times when X fades into the background; other times X will be very much in the foreground. The acute pain of early death is no reason to try to blot out their memory. You will still remember X in months and years to come, even as you seek to move on with your lives...."

"Leaves should not fall in early summer. Winter should not follow on the heels of Spring. At such a time, the inevitable question is, 'Why did this happen?' But there is no answer. X died not because of anything you did, or failed to do – but because we live in a world subject to nature's vagaries. We might as well ask why a particular leaf on a tree failed to unfurl, or was blown away at a particular time. We are subject, like all living things, to nature's mishaps. The glory of one life is not that it endures for ever, but that, for a time, it included so much beauty. Our habit of measuring the worth of a life by its duration is not a good one. As a Zen proverb says: 'The morning glory, which blooms for an hour, differs not at heart from the giant pine that lives for a thousand years'.

"Ben Jonson, who lost a child in infancy, wrote this poem, *'It is not growing like a tree........'*. X was the fair lily which bloomed for a day – beautiful and perfect, as only babies can be. Even the briefest moments have enduring value. X's short life is to be cherished for what it was. For a time, s/he brought joy and anticipation – and in return experienced your tenderness and love.

"Today it is natural to feel the rawness of grief, but perhaps Kahlil Gibran is right when he says that joy and sorrow are woven fine: our ability to feel deep pain may yet heighten our capacity to feel deep joy. The best answer to death is the continuing affirmation of life. While death comes to us all, sooner or later, our lives, with all their joys and sorrows, are ours to shape. This life on earth is all we know, so let us reaffirm our commitment to make the most of the one precious life we each have – and may this be X's legacy to us."

Words for the Committal

"It is said that we are made of stardust; that when we die, the molecules that make up our bodies return to the earth to be reborn, in the rosebud and fledgling bird. So gently, reverently, and with love, we commit the body of X to the embrace of Mother Earth, which sustains and regenerates all life. Our thoughts, our feelings, our longings, go with X as we say our goodbyes. Fly little one, away from pain; immune to the changes, chances, and hazards of this world. Be at peace – held safe in our memory and our love. And for you who remain, may peace and strength and understanding grow from this sorrow, in due season. May you hold on to what is good and true and beautiful, in faith that happier days will come again."

Case Study 2: Funeral after Suicide

Several years ago, a member of my congregation, with three sisters and parents closely connected to the chapel but not members, discovered that a very good friend had attempted to take his own life. This friend, let's call him John, was also a very dear friend of the other members of the family. After the suicide attempt, John arrived in hospital seriously unwell and died soon after. Not only were the family shocked by the attempted suicide: they were also trying to give him support in hospital after it and before his death. Uppermost in their minds was the question: how might they have done something to prevent it from happening? They were tormented by that thought and blamed themselves for not sufficiently recognising how unhappy he was.

Talking about a person's death with family and friends before the funeral is probably as important, if not more important, than the funeral itself. And this is true in all circumstances. But in the case of a suicide, it is such a vital task when the emotions of those who cared for and loved the person are raw with grief. Bringing them together to speak of those feelings and bearing witness to them can bring some measure of peace and acceptance. In this case those who cared were not his own family, from whom he was estranged, but the family of the member of my congregation.

A funeral service is both for honouring a person's life and for providing spiritual support for those who feel the loss most deeply. But in the case of a suicide, those feeling the loss often carry the burden of not having done enough to prevent it. Bringing them into a circle of quietness, where the clamour of self-judgement can be eased and where their own sense of failure, regret, and guilt is allowed to be spoken of, is a great gift to give them at such a difficult time.

I recall asking those people who attended the service to create a circle of love and compassion in their minds. Although we could not create it physically, we were able to imagine it. An encircling prayer is part of the Celtic Christian tradition. It asks for protection from discouragement and despair and brings with it a healing closeness.

There are beautiful words in both *Great Occasions* (edited by Carl Seaburg, 1983) and in *Celebrating Life* (compiled and edited by Andrew Hill, 1993). There will be other, more contemporary, resources. Many of them take us right to the heart of suffering, like these words of Peter Raible (*Great Occasions*): "We come bearing our grief, deeply shaken and bruised by this death, asking ourselves what we might have done to prevent it." They are words that help us to prepare mentally and spiritually for this most difficult of services, and they can be adapted as we see fit.

The idea of a circle came from *In Memoriam – A Guide to Modern Funeral and Memorial Services* (edited by Edward Searle, 1993). One of the services began with these words:

> *Come into this circle of loss*
> *Come into this circle of compassion*
> *Come into this circle of memory*
> *Come into this circle of love.*

Case Study 3: Suicide by a Veteran

I was asked by a veterans' organisation to lead a funeral for a person whom I had met, but did not know very well. He had committed suicide, and his parents were in deep shock and wanted to see me. I went with a veteran who knew the parents.

The story that was presented was that he was a loving family man whose partner had recently taken the children and refused to let either the deceased or his parents see them. The parents were in shock and fearful that they would lose access to their grandchildren. They did not know that there had been accusations of incest until the day before the funeral, when the police showed them the suicide note.

His veteran friends were also deeply distressed at his death and thought that the loss of access to his children had triggered his suicide. There was an added dimension because a couple of the other veterans were talking about him having the 'guts' to go through with it, so we had to talk them down from considering a 'copycat' act.

The day before the funeral, one of the veterans discovered the story and told me about it on the morning of the funeral. The funeral service needed a rapid re-write, to leave out the claims about his being a loving father. Most of the 200 veterans who attended the funeral did not know of the child-abuse allegations.

On reflection, I realise I should have asked to speak with the estranged partner to confirm whether the children would be coming, and what if anything she would want to say. I accepted the parents' version of the "wicked" mother denying them access to their grandchildren. I suspect that I would have been put straight in no time. My advice is, when people are being cut out of the story, look behind the initial explanation and seek to verify claims by asking the other party. It may be tough, but in a difficult case it may avoid embarrassment.

One of the other veterans was feeling deep remorse because the subject of paedophilia had come up on the day when the victim had taken his own life. This man had described in graphic detail what he would do to a paedophile, and subsequently he felt that he had driven the man to take his life. Other veterans had their 'brave man' image dashed. I did a lot of listening.

I stayed in touch with the parents, who had gone away for a long holiday to salve their wounds, and I remembered them especially on the anniversary of the death.

4 Induction of Ministers or Lay Leaders

Introduction

Appropriate local leadership is a vital element of the Unitarian and Free Christian congregational network. Differing levels of financial viability and support mechanisms will help to determine the type of leadership available. For many, the ideal or hoped-for leader will be a minister or lay leader trained to an appropriate standard by our approved Unitarian institutions, to an agreed level of competence.

The successful completion of training, and the arrival at a congregation for the first time (at several points in most careers) are moments of celebration and thankfulness. Traditionally, British Unitarians have celebrated the start of a new ministry with an Induction Service, where the minister and new congregation call upon each other for necessary support, guidance, and commitment. These services are important in bringing together the congregation, and they provide an opportunity to engage the wider community too. For many, the induction provides a first chance to meet with local politicians, community leaders, and fellow clergy. A well-constructed induction service will provide a valuable window on the work of the minister, the congregation, and the wider Unitarian community.

With an increasing number of local lay leaders becoming skilled in congregational leadership, it is important to recognise the formal acceptance of such a leader into a new position. It is more likely that a lay leader will already be well known to the congregation, and he or she is most likely to have been a member of the congregation itself. That does not, however, diminish the importance of recognising this transition and new beginning. This chapter looks at how induction services might be considered and constructed.

Purpose and preparation

An induction service is usually held at the start of a new ministry – but not only as a one-off event for a newly recognised minister or lay leader, but for every new start at a new congregation. The purpose is threefold: to welcome a newly appointed minister or lay leader to the congregation and, if appropriate, to the local area; for the minister or lay leader to make a public commitment to the congregation to serve them to the best of their ability; and for the congregation to make a public commitment to support the minister or lay leader.

The induction service is arranged and created jointly by the new incumbent, the congregation, and a second minister or local Unitarian congregational leader who will be asked by the new incumbent to guide the service. This is usually a friend or mentor. In addition, the service will usually include other Unitarian ministers and leaders. who are invited to read or give a 'charge' to the congregation (more on this later).

Attenders at an induction service will vary, but it is usual to invite all the congregation; members of the minister's or lay leader's family; members and ministers of local Unitarian and Free Christian congregations; the President or Chief Officer of the General Assembly of Unitarian and Free Christian Churches; local clergy and leaders from other faith groups; the Mayor or other local government leader; the local MP; and local media. The total number invited will of course be dependent on the size of the church or meeting house, but it is good to make the service as broad and inclusive a celebration as possible.

Induction service at a glance

Music

An induction service is a public event, perhaps drawing many people to the church or meeting house who may not regularly attend our services, or may not know much about Unitarianism. This is therefore a chance to present us in the very best light. Consider live music if you can – played on the piano, organ, cello, etc. – or, if recorded music is the only option, take care in choosing something appropriate, rather than the first track on the 'Easy Listening Classics' CD lying nearby.

Opening words and chalice lighting

Opening words should be spoken by the service leader. This is a time to create a sacred space, to recognise the transition from a secular place to a place of worship and sanctuary. Stillness and silence might follow these, to help people to settle into the space and to feel more comfortable. You might use words such as these:

> *Welcome to this place today.*
> *We gather to worship, we gather to welcome,*
> *We gather to continue the story of this congregation.*
>
> *As we settle in stillness and silence,*
> *May we be reminded of all those who have been in this place before us.*
> *May we feel the presence of all around us, joining as one in sacred celebration.*
> *May we understand our place as the forebears of the generations to come.*
>
> *We gather as one, with our own stories, our own traditions.*
>
> *We gather to welcome our new Minister [or Lay Leader] with love in our hearts.*

Induction service at a glance

This is a good time to light a Chalice flame too, with simple words such as these:

> *As we light this Chalice flame, a symbol of our Unitarian faith and commitment around the world, we settle now to stillness, to become part of this place today.*

Words of welcome

Welcoming words should be spoken by either the Chair or leader of the congregation, or by the person chosen to lead the whole service. This is an opportunity to welcome all to the place of worship, to describe how and why the service is taking place, and to introduce some of the key people in the service.

This is also an opportunity for a local politician or the Mayor to offer words of welcome too. This could be left until later in the service, but placing it here allows the remainder of the service to be focused more fully on Unitarian and Free Christian worship.

Presentation of the new minister

It is quite usual for a representative of the General Assembly of Unitarian and Free Christian Churches to be invited to an induction service, and this is an opportunity to hear from them as they bring the greetings of the Assembly to the gathered congregation and welcome the appointment and calling of the minister or lay leader.

Opening hymn

An induction service is a time of joy and celebration, and the opening hymn will set the tone for the service ahead. This is also an opportunity for the gathered congregation to sing as one, perhaps for the first time.

Induction of Ministers or Lay Leaders

Induction service at a glance

Given that there may be people present who are not used to a Unitarian service or hymns, you may want to choose a well-known hymn, or perhaps Unitarian words set to a well-known tune.

Prayer

A time for reflection and prayer. This might be led by another Unitarian minister – either a friend or mentor of the new leader, or a local minister.

Readings

The choice of readers and readings is important. This is an opportunity to allow the Chair and/or another member of the congregation to play a part, or another minister or lay leader. Alternatively, a member of the new minister's family, or perhaps a godparent, could take this role.

As with any Unitarian service, the reading can be chosen from many different sources. If a Biblical reading is deemed appropriate or desirable, a passage from Isaiah 6:1–8 might be appropriate.

Charge to the Congregation

The role of a congregational minister or lay leader can be tiring, frustrating, and exhausting. While self-care will be important, there is a need for the new congregation to recognise and accept that it has a role to play in supporting the minister or lay leader. The Charge to the Congregation is a formal delegation of responsibility to the congregation, usually by a more senior minister or leader, ideally a senior minister already known and respected by the congregation, or someone with a particular sense of care for the new leader – perhaps a mentor or college tutor. The charge usually lasts five minutes and is best written anew by the minister who gives it. The key points to be addressed are that the health and welfare of the minister or lay leader are paramount to the new relationship, and that a healthy recognition of boundaries and responsibilities will be necessary. It is increasingly recognised as important to stress that it is the minister or lay leader who has been called, not her or his partner or spouse, and the congregation should recognise that distinction. A good-humoured piece will more likely engage the congregation and remind them of their duties.

Music

By this point, the stage has been set for the formal welcome. This is a good opportunity for a piece of quiet, reflective music, either recorded or played by a live musician.

Induction by the congregation

To formally 'induct' the leader to the new congregation, and responding to the Charge made upon it, the Chair or Secretary of the congregation may take this opportunity to call the new minister or lay leader to the front. The Chair, or Secretary, should say some words of their own choosing, welcoming the minister or lay leader to the congregation and promising to build a strong working relationship.

The Chair should conclude by asking the gathered congregation – which will include regular congregation members and others – to repeat a promise to the minister or lay leader. It is best to write this afresh for each occasion, although something along the following lines would be suitable:

> *We, the Congregation and Friends of the Downton Unitarian and Free Christian Meeting House, choose to induct you as our [Minister / Lay Leader].*

Induction service at a glance

> *We pledge, as individuals and as a congregation, to join with you in the work and celebration of a free, compassionate, and loving religion, recognising the worth of every person and the oneness of humanity, the Earth, and the Universe.*

Response by the new minister or lay leader

At this point, the new minister or lay leader might respond to the formal Induction with a simple statement of acceptance, and a commitment to work together with the congregation in a mutually supportive way.

Charge to the Minister or Lay Leader

The Charge is usually given by a senior minister – perhaps known to the congregation or the new minister. Or it could be given by the minister's tutor, if this is his or her first role as a minister.

The Charge to the Minister or Lay Leader, in line with the previous Charge to the Congregation, again usually lasts approximately five minutes and is best written anew by the minister giving it. The key points to be addressed are the role of the minister or lay leader as a servant leader; the need to recognise their strengths, and to acknowledge what they still need to develop; to commit to working collaboratively with the congregation and the local community as a witness to liberal religion in the area. Again, the health and welfare of the new leader are paramount, and the Charge should include a reminder that the minister or lay leader needs to balance work with time to recharge and re-energise.

Induction service at a glance

Prayers

As the service begins to draw to a close, a time of prayer for the new ministry, for the congregation, for the local community, and the well-being of all is appropriate. As this follows the Charge to the Minister (or Lay Leader), this is a good opportunity for the new leader to lead an element of worship.

Hymn

A rousing hymn to finish worship will bring the gathered ministers, guests, and congregation together once more in a single voice.

Benediction

A short benediction, pronounced by the service leader, completes the service.

5 Ordination of Ministers

Introduction

Ordination of ministers has not been a regular practice in British Unitarian congregations for many years. There has been a tendency to associate ordination with setting the minister above the lay community, and to see it as a reference to the established Christian tradition from which our Unitarian forebears dissented, rather than seeing it as a 'setting apart', which is very different and probably more acceptable. With roots in the established Church, it is certainly the case that Unitarian and Free Christian ministers are part of the longer tradition of ordained leaders, and there has been some discussion about reconsidering ordination in a wider sense: with an eye to the past, and in recognition of necessary changes to bring our dissenting message to the fore, some ordination services have been held recently, and there is a growing interest in restoring this rite to British Unitarianism. This chapter therefore seeks to understand and recognise this growing call, and to suggest some resources to support ministers and others looking to create such a service.

Purpose and preparation

Ordination is one of the sacraments of the Christian Church. While its origins in structure are uncertain, most theologians trace it back to Jesus' calling of the twelve disciples, and their subsequent mission to go out and call more spiritual leaders. In this conferring of authority from Jesus to the disciples, and the subsequent continued delegation of authority, Christian ordination recognises the calling of peers by peers, and the transference or sharing of the Holy Spirit through an apostolic or priestly connection.

It is the case that those trained and recognised by Unitarians can generally trace a line back to those ordained in the Christian tradition before 1662 (as those ordained welcomed the next generation, and the next and the next....): hence the continued and appropriate use of the style 'Reverend'. Unitarian ministers are considered by many as an aspect of that original 'Ordering' that ordination recognises; it is still the case that Unitarian ministers are recognised by their peers, continuing the tradition. Formal ordination of ministers in the British Unitarian and Free Christian movement is, however, not common, partly due to its overt link to the established Christian Church, but also to avoid a suggestion of 'setting above' – consciously or unconsciously. Widespread ordination of British Unitarian ministers ceased in the early nineteenth century.

For many newly qualified ministers, the recognition has been accorded jointly by the Valediction Service – provided by the College responsible for training ministers – and the Welcome to the Roll of Unitarian and Free Christian Ministers, usually held as part of the Annual Service at the Annual Meetings of the General Assembly. However, there is an increased interest in ordination as a separate and unique element in the minister's public acceptance and commitment, although this will remain discretionary.

An ordination service, as opposed to the induction for a new incumbent, provides a visible celebration of the successful training, recognition, and calling of a minister to service and to sacrifice. It is also a test of the credentials and acceptability of an individual into ministry, and it should be considered also as a spiritual rite of passage: many newly qualified ministers will see it as a sanctifying moment in their calling.

A key element of ordination is the 'laying on of hands' by other ministers, demonstrating a visible and physical connection to peers and to the past. There is some Biblical indication of this when Barnabas and Saul are blessed and sent out by the Apostles (as recorded in the Book of Acts), and there are more direct references in the First Letter of Paul to Timothy and The Letter to the Hebrews, but the formal element of the service has developed more through the later establishment of the Christian Church. For Unitarians, to ordain with the laying on of hands therefore risks sending a visible and physical message that ministers are in some way set apart. The impression might be softened with words emphasising that this is a bond of collegiality, or alternatively those invited to 'lay on hands' might include people other than trained ministers or clergy of other faiths. It is a risk that requires mitigation.

A second vital element of traditional ordination is the putting of questions to the new minister regarding his or her faith. This forms in effect a 'Confession of Faith' and would usually involve, for example, acceptance of Christ as Saviour and a declared belief in the truth of Scripture. For Unitarians, with an approach to faith that requires the acceptance of reason and rejection of dogma, a Confession of Faith is likely to prove more personal. For example, the traditional questions on the inerrancy of the Bible, and the importance of the Lord's Supper, are generally inappropriate or, if used, might solicit very different answers.

Unitarians believe in the ministry of all (as indeed does the Christian Church), and it is important to ensure that there is no indication in ordination services that the newly trained minister is in any way superior to the laity or other office holders. Rather, the ceremony is (for Unitarians at least) a recognition of a commitment to become a servant leader, and a rite of passage for this significant moment in a minister's life.

If it is intended to hold an ordination service, consideration will need to be given to the most appropriate location. For many, this might be the 'home' congregation of a newly trained minister, recognising the support that the individual has received in formation, and recalling a time when ministers were ordained or chosen from within congregations before being sent out to new congregations.

Those invited to the service might include the home congregation, representatives of the College at which the ordinand trained, Unitarian and Free Christian ministers from local congregations or from farther afield, and local clergy and faith leaders. The home congregation might wish also to use the opportunity to inform local media about the event.

Care needs to be taken when choosing a minister to lead the service. Since there is no formal seniority within the Unitarian ministry (we have, for example, no Bishops), consideration might be given to choosing a long-serving minister, perhaps one with a formal connection to the congregation or the ordinand.

Ordination service at a glance

Music

An ordination service is a public event, perhaps drawing many people to the church or meeting house who may not regularly attend our services or might not know much about Unitarianism. This is therefore a chance to present the movement in the very best light. Consider including good live music – played on the piano, organ, or other instrument – but if an appropriate piece of recorded music is used, make sure that the sound quality is technically very good, and the choice of music is appropriate for the occasion.

Opening words and chalice lighting

Opening words should be spoken by the minister chosen to lead the service (see above). This is a time to create a sacred space, to recognise the transition from a secular place to a place of worship and sanctuary. Stillness and silence might follow, to help people to settle into the space and to feel more comfortable. Words such as these might be used:

> *Welcome to this place today.*
> *We gather to worship, we gather to welcome,*
> *We gather to witness and welcome this key point on the journey for [ORDINAND'S NAME]*
>
> *As we settle in stillness and silence,*
> *May we be reminded of all those who have brought ministry in all its forms.*
> *May we feel the presence of all around us, joining as one in sacred celebration.*
>
> *May we recognise and develop the role that each of us has to make this world a better place.*

Ordination service at a glance

> *We gather as one, with our own stories, our own traditions.*
> *We gather to support [ORDINAND] on this next step in his/her life.*

This is a good time to light a chalice flame too, with some simple words:

> *As we light this chalice flame, a symbol of our Unitarian faith and commitment around the world,*
>
> *We settle now to stillness, to become part of this place today.*

Words of welcome

Welcoming words provide an opportunity to welcome all to the place of worship, to describe how and why the service is taking place, and introduce some of the key people in the service.

This is also an opportunity for a local politician or the Mayor to offer words of welcome too. This could be left until later in the service, but placing it here ensures that the remainder of the service is focused more fully on Unitarian and Free Christian worship.

Presentation of the ordinand

It is usual for a representative of the General Assembly of Unitarian and Free Christian Churches to be invited to an ordination service, and this is an opportunity to hear from them as they bring the greetings of the Assembly to the gathered congregation, and welcome the appointment and calling of the minister. Given that the ordinand is, at this point, newly placed on the General Assembly's Roll of Unitarian and Free Christian Ministers, it might be appropriate for a declaration to be made, confirming that the ordinand has reached the agreed level of competence and has demonstrated a clear and purposeful calling to the Unitarian ministry.

Ordination service at a glance

Opening hymn

An ordination service is a time of joy and celebration, and the opening hymn will set the tone for the service ahead. This is also an opportunity for the gathered congregation to sing as one, perhaps for the first time. Given that there may be people present who are not used to a Unitarian service or hymns, you may want to choose a well-known hymn, or perhaps one with Unitarian words set to a well-known tune.

Prayer

A time for reflection and prayer. This might be led by another Unitarian minister – either a friend or mentor of the new minister, or a local minister.

Readings

Choice of readers and readings is important. This is an opportunity to involve recently qualified ministers, or perhaps family or friends of the ordinand. Additionally, the Ministerial Tutor from the college at which the ordinand trained may be a possibility.

As with any Unitarian service, the reading can be chosen from many different sources. If a Biblical reading is deemed appropriate or desirable, a passage from Isaiah 6:1–8 might be appropriate.

Test *or* Confession of Faith

There is no single, agreed Test or Confession across all churches or denominations. However, in a more traditional Christian setting, the Confession of Faith will usually accord with the creedal beliefs of the Church, the infallibility of Scripture, agreed Articles of Faith, and self-less commitment to the service of others.

Ordination service at a glance

For Unitarians, such an approach would be counter to the ethos of freedom of belief and test by conscience. If such an element were to be included, therefore, it is vital that it reflects the personal faith of the ordinand and, of equal importance, the values of the Unitarian movement. The questions and words of confession should be worked on carefully, as it is an opportunity for the ordinand to confirm his or her commitment to a vocation of ministry.

The following are some sample questions:

Celebrant: *Do you accept and seek to demonstrate the inherent worth and dignity of every person?*

Ordinand: *I do.*

Celebrant: *Do you promise to seek the peace and unity of the Unitarian movement, to bring harmony where there is discord, and to work for understanding and acceptance with those both within and without the movement?*

Ordinand: *I do.*

Celebrant: *Do you resolve to be inclusive in your ministry, to accept the personal nature and truth of faith and belief, and to welcome those of all faiths as part of the universal human family?*

Ordinand: *I do.*

Celebrant: *Do you call upon your inner strength to help you strive to live a peaceful and worthwhile life, serving the needs of the poor, bringing relief to the oppressed, and working as an advocate for those in need?*

Ordinand: *I do.*

Ordination service at a glance

Stillness

Recognising the personal yet public commitment to a life of servant leader made in the Confession of Faith, it is good to guide the congregation to a time of stillness and reflection for perhaps two minutes. This can be followed by music to continue the reflection.

Laying on of hands

As mentioned in the introduction to this chapter, the Laying on of Hands as a means of ordaining a spiritual leader is rooted deeply in the Christian tradition and Biblical instruction. Generally conducted by other members of the clergy, this ritual has demonstrated a sense of welcome and acceptance as part of the 'Order' of spiritual leadership. From a Unitarian perspective, there is a significant risk here of alienating the congregation from the clergy, or implying a separation of the ordinand from the 'ordinary people'. To overcome this, and to make clear the Unitarian principles of inclusion and equality, it might be appropriate to create a new approach. As an example, the ordinand might be asked to stand or sit in the centre of the church, while people come forward to lay hands on them.

An approach that would respect both the tradition of the sacrament and the creativity of the evolving Unitarian faith might be to ask representatives of the Unitarian clergy first to place hands on the ordinand. This might be followed by invited representatives from other churches and faith groups, to be followed by people from the gathered congregation, and representatives of local institutions and civic bodies.

The laying on of hands represents a connection to all, and to something greater than the sum of all parts. By joining with many other humans, each unique and each representing a different journey in life, this is the moment of ordination to religious ministry. Here are some suggested words:

> *Spirit of Life, contained within each of us, and greater than us all, by the laying on of hands we ordain and appoint [FULL NAME] to the office of sacred ministry, committing him/her to a life of leader and servant, in the Order of all that is Holy.*
>
> *We give thanks that (FULL NAME) has heard and responded to the call to ministry. May he/she be for each of us all a source of strength and inspiration, that with him/her we may share in the ministry of all that is holy, seeking reconciliation for those who are divided, peace and healing for those who are broken or live in fear, and justice for those who are oppressed.*

Prayers

As the service begins to draw to a close, a time of prayer for the new ministry, for the congregation, for the local community, and the well-being of all is appropriate. As this follows the Charge to the Minister, this is a good opportunity for the minister to lead an element of worship.

Hymn

A rousing hymn to finish worship will bring the gathered ministers and congregation together once more in a single voice.

Benediction

A short benediction, offered by the service leader, completes the ceremony.

6 Membership Services

Introduction

The notion of congregational membership is often the last thing that people will be looking for when they first cross the threshold of a Unitarian or Free Christian church or meeting house. For many, the appeal is the promise of a faith that allows free expression and the avoidance of creedal conformity, so the idea that there might be a community approach that could support such a position comes as a surprise to some.

A Unitarian congregation can only exist through the collective efforts of its members. Ministers and lay leaders are no doubt essential in most contexts, but the congregation is the purpose of the community: without the congregation there will be no point in the existence of a minister or lay leader. The congregation is also the continuum that links the past, the present, and the future of the religious community in question, and the congregation exists to provide a space for all searchers to experience the freedom of the Unitarian approach.

Membership of a Unitarian congregation is not dependent on subscription to a creed or dogma, nor is it a deliberate attempt to persuade an individual to abandon their personal spiritual exploration. Instead, in a Unitarian context, membership provides a visible and personal commitment to the preservation of the congregation, and thus the continued provision of a safe and supportive space for future explorers. For the individual, an invitation into membership brings a sense of being needed and appreciated; for the congregation, an acceptance of an invitation to membership provides reassurance of continued commitment and communal effort to maintain its existence.

Membership invitations vary from place to place and will often have roots in the particular congregational history. Some congregations will offer membership to individuals almost immediately after a first attendance, others will wait for six months or a year to allow both congregation and individual to determine whether they are right for one another. While both sides must be happy with the idea of membership, congregations are encouraged to welcome all: new people will often bring new ideas, and without new ideas and change, congregations will eventually weaken and die.

Membership services are often held annually, or perhaps half-yearly, and are an opportunity for the new member to make a formal and visible commitment to the congregation, and for the congregation to welcome the new member and offer the hand of friendship and community. It is not unusual for several new members to be welcomed at the same time. Alternatively, some congregations may wish to welcome new members on a more ad-hoc basis, welcoming new members individually as they accept an invitation.

Membership services are best held as part of a regular Sunday service – or an anniversary service, if one is held. Making it a small part of a more regular service increases the sense of connection and commitment to the routine activities of the congregation, which is surely the aim and purpose of membership. The following suggested approach is therefore not a 'stand-alone' service: instead it is designed to be inserted into a more regular service, perhaps after the sermon and before the final hymn. It is essential that you talk through the plan and the wording with the new member before the service: he or she must feel comfortable and engaged, and consultation is a crucial element to any successful partnership.

Membership Services

Welcoming a new member – as part of a regular Sunday service

Introduction

Announce to the congregation that there is now to be a special part of the service, where a new member, or new members, will be welcomed into the fellowship of the congregation.

Ask the new member(s) to step forward to the front, and also call forward a leading lay person – the Chair or Secretary of the Committee perhaps.

Statement of principles

It is good to begin with a restatement of the congregation's statement of belief, or vision. If no formal text exists, all congregations are strongly encouraged to work together to define one – but for the time being try to write something yourself that will reflect the freedom and commitment of the congregation. Here is an example:

> *This meeting house and its congregation have been here present for over 200 years, and the congregation that meets here today is a continuation of that original gathering; a living stream of dedicated individuals committed to the loving community of this place and its ideals. The beliefs of this congregation have evolved to reflect the ideas and ideals of its members. This congregation is a representative community, sharing its commitment to free and inquiring religion, and the pursuit of social justice. This congregation is not bound by creed or dogma, and it welcomes new members, to broaden its understanding of the world, and to offer fellowship and support.*
>
> *This congregation recognises the inherent worth and dignity of all people, with respect for the interdependent web of all existence. The members of this congregation may differ in their individual religious*

Welcoming a new member – as part of a regular Sunday service

beliefs or spiritual path, but they unite in pursuit of a peaceful world where love for all creation will help to ease hardship and inequality. This congregation believes that we must all play a part in delivering a better world.

Charge to the new member, and their response

At this point, a 'Charge' to the new member, to make explicit the requirements and expectations on both sides, is important. The following suggested words borrow heavily from Andrew Hill's book *Celebrating Life* and bring a welcome element of humour to this happy event.

> *BECKY, it is not difficult to join this congregation. There are no exams, no secret votes, no external qualifications required. And the material rewards are few. As Unitarians, we do not even offer eternal salvation.*
>
> *In fact, your act of membership will probably bring you, and most likely already has brought you, more requests for service and support than it will be the cause for rewards and statements of appreciation.*
>
> *But above all else, we ask that you make to this community a very special gift: the gift of your individual ideas and your sensitive ideals. I charge you, in your act of membership, to share with us your creative thoughts, your vital experiences in life, your questions, your doubts, and your discoveries of all the ways in which life affects you and those people and principles that matter most to you.*
>
> *BECKY, will you support the life and worship of this congregation, uphold its principles and purposes, and make every effort to live them out, not just in your own life but in the life of the world about you?*
>
> *RESPONSE: I will.*

Membership Services

Welcoming a new member – as part of a regular Sunday service

There then follows a Charge to the congregation:

> Will you, the present members and friends of this Unitarian community, welcome BECKY to the life and work of this congregation and support her as a member of our community?
>
> RESPONSE: We will.

Formal welcome from the congregation

At this point, it would be good for the Chair or Secretary of the congregation – representing the membership rather than the minister or lay leader – to welcome the new member formally, followed by a joint welcome from the congregation, speaking together. Here are some suggested words:

[The Chair or Secretary:]

> In the name of this congregation, I welcome you into our fellowship, and offer you the hand of friendship on behalf of all the congregation.
>
> [Shake Becky's hand]

[Chair or Secretary]:

> Will all here present please join me in the words on the reverse of your service sheet:
>
> We, the members and friends of LONGFIELD UNITARIANS, welcome and congratulate you, BECKY, as a new member in the search for truth. We welcome your commitment to share our concern for a better world, and our free inquiry into meaning and belief. We look to share our strength and support with yours, and we delight in the promise of a future we might shape together.

Welcoming a new member – as part of a regular Sunday service

[Minister or Lay Leader]:

I know that many other people will want to extend the hand of fellowship to BECKY after the service. May the relationship we have all recognised here today, on the first day of the next 300 years for this congregation, be a source of strength, joy, and courage to us all.

Return to the main service

Annex A: Words for Child Namings

A call to everyone present

Let us teach our children that their minds and their bodies are worthy of worship, and should be nurtured, fed with living waters and spiritual nourishment.

Let us teach them to feel the joy of belonging to a community of living, loving souls, connecting at the very root of their being.

Let us teach them how to grow into strong, independent people, living in honesty and integrity, but always aware that they are surrounded and supported by friends.

Let us teach them to feel the pain of the earth when we hurt it, and to dance with joy for each opening flower, and each newborn life.

Let us teach them to live respectfully towards others, but never to feel diminished by others – if we claim equality for everybody else, we must be strong enough to claim it for ourselves also.

Let us teach them that life will bring pain and sorrow as well as pleasure and joy, but that both good times and bad times should be valued for what they can teach us.

Let us teach them to live and to love with every fibre of their being, and to let them know that they are loved.

Anna Jarvis

....

Calls to the parents

The coming of a child into a family is a time for rejoicing.
When a child comes into a family,

It is a time for rejoicing and thanksgiving.

It is a time for hope.

Today we are here to welcome .... to her/his forever family,
To a place where he/she will be safe and free to grow fully,
Loved and cherished, not only by her/his parents
But by the whole family of which she/he is now fully part.

You have been blessed by the coming of this child into your lives.
There will be many who will not understand the challenges you all face.
Your task is to be the parents this child needs,
For her/him to feel loved, safe, respected, whole,
Secure in herself/himself in order for her/him to fulfil his/her potential in life.

And so I ask you now to pledge your unconditional love, support, and care for her/him,
To love and cherish her/him and to build in her/him the sense of her/his own worth,
To lead her/him, by example, in the paths of kindness and love, generosity and joy.
Will you so pledge?

Parent/s: *We/I do.*

Celia Cartwright

__ & __ in bringing this child to be welcomed through this gathering into the fellowship of faith, you acknowledge that he/she is the gift of God entrusted to your love and nurture, and you declare your desire and purpose to bring him/her up according to his/her need for loving care, and your determination to guide him/her with understanding, compassion, and the best of your love.

According to the best of your ability, do you then promise to lead him/her in the way of truth and honesty, to treat him/her always with justice, to support his/her education, always offering him/her the best of your wisdom in guidance and advice, and always to use words carefully, to speak well of him/her, to encourage him/her, above all by demonstrating to him/her that he/she is loved.

Response: *We do.*

Jo James

A call to family and friends

The gathered family and guests are invited to read together:

We as your family WELCOME and name you *[full name............]*.
We promise to nurture you and help you to discover who you are and what you believe.
We will value your individuality, uniqueness, and talents.
Welcome to the world, *[first name]*!

Elizabeth Harley

Calls to the godparents

.... and .... [name of godparents], you are entering into a treasured commitment to .... as godparents.

Will you offer your support and friendship in the years to come, encouraging .... in all her/his life challenges and changes, helping her/him to find all that is real and healthy, and walking alongside .... in her/his journey of growing, learning, and being?

We will.

Will you support .... and .... [parents/carers of the child] in the transformative, uplifting, and at times tough responsibilities of parenthood over the years to come – and offer them your understanding and compassion?

Will you be there for them in their experiences of life, in difficult times and joyful times, on days of struggle and days of laughter?

We will.

Will you offer encouragement to .... in her/his quest for meaning and wisdom and wholeness in this mysterious world of wonder?

We will.

I am going to invite you to light a candle each to symbolise the light and warmth and presence you will bring to .... and this family over the years to come, and to remind us all that the flickering flame of love is so central to all our lives.

John Harley

Will you, the godparents of (name), promise to be a positive force in her/his life, to love her/him, guide her/him, and help her/him when she/he needs it as a child, and then support her/his choices in adult life?

Will you be a champion for her/his rights and freedoms and encourage her/him to act with kindness and compassion?

Answer: *We will.*

Elizabeth Harley

•••

Do you recognise your responsibility to nurture, support, and develop __ 's upbringing, encouraging their sense of wonder and awe at the world around them, their gratitude for the gifts they have been given, their duty to the talents they will develop – and will you encourage their education, insight, and moral discernment?

Will you be close to them in spirit, no matter how far away in miles, providing them with a shoulder to rely on and an ear to listen whatever their difficulties?

Response: *"We will".*

Jo James

•••

Naming prayers

In the name of the one true God, whose nature we have learned is love, I baptise you and bid you welcome; a word that simply means, 'well ... come'.

For you are indeed well come into the home and family where you will live and grow, loved and cared for by your parents [and sisters and brothers].

Well come, into the wider community where you will live and take your place, represented here by your godparents, relatives, friends, and members of this congregation.

Well come, to your place on earth, [with your brothers and sisters] as a member of God's world-wide human family.

May you know God's love, may you know God's truth; and may you be something good in this world.

And to this prayer, to this blessing, let us all say, Amen.

John Midgley

....

[NAME] I baptise you with water, symbol of your purity.
I touch your eyes that you may see beauty.
I touch your ears that you may hear sounds of joy and love.
I touch your mouth that you may speak your truth without condemnation.
I touch your brow that your thoughts may be kind and unfettered by fears.
May you know you are a blessed child of the universe,
May your life be filled with wonder and acceptance.
Amen.

Celia Cartwright

....

You are baptised with water as a symbol of the common life which is in you and in the world about you. In the name of that spirit which was in Jesus, we welcome you to the community of life, to the possibility of faith, and the promise of everything which is beautiful and true and good.

May every blessing be upon you, and may love be with you,
may the face of heaven shine upon you,
and all creation be gracious to you,
and may you live in peace.
Amen

Jo James

....

I want you to be happy.
I want you to fill your heart with feelings of wonder and to be full of courage and hope.

I want you to have the type of friendship that is a treasure – and the kind of love that is beautiful for ever.
I wish you contentment: the sweet, quiet, inner kind that comes around and never goes away.
I want you to have hopes and have them all come true.

I want you to have a real understanding of how unique and rare you truly are.
I want to remind you that the sun may disappear for a while, but it never forgets to shine. May the words you listen to say the things you need to hear. And may a cheerful face lovingly look back at you when you happen to glance in your mirror.
I wish you the insight to see your inner and outer beauty.

I wish you sweet dreams.
I want you to have times when you feel like singing and dancing and laughing out loud.
I want you to be able to make your good times better, and your hard times easier to handle.
I wish I could find a way to tell you – in untold ways – how important you are to me.

Of all the things I'll be wishing for, wherever you are and whatever I may do, there will never be a day in my life when I won't be wishing for the best ... for you.

Anonymous

Annex A: Words for Child Namings

Spirit of Life and Love,
We give thanks for this day
On which we welcome .... into this family and this community.

We give thanks that though we do not live in a perfect world,
And there are those whose lives are wounded by events beyond their control,
There are those too whose hearts lead them to love and to heal.

As the beloved child of this/these parent/s,
May she/he know that she/he is loved.
May she/he know that she/he is safe.
May she/he now grow into herself/himself,
Strong and bold, or quiet and gentle,
Free to be who and what she/he wants to be.

And may this/these parent/s
Find strength and purpose in his/her/their task
To nurture, support, and love his/her/their child
Into confident maturity.

Blessed is the parent in the gift of a child to cherish.
Blessed is the child blessed with the gift of unconditional love.
Blessed is the family where understanding and love blossom.

May this family be so blessed.
Amen

Celia Cartwright

....

Responsive prayers

In a society torn apart by violence and division, we recognise that what unites us is much more important than what divides us. We recognise our responsibility to work for a society where diversity is recognised and celebrated, with people from different traditions living together in mutual understanding and respect.

All: Welcome into our hearts and into our lives.

In a world where the misuse of resources by the rich destroys the lives of the poor and threatens the future of the earth, we recognise that we have only borrowed the world from our children, and that it is our responsibility to both conserve and share the world's resources so that they can be enjoyed by all the world's children for generations to come.

All: Welcome into our hearts and into our lives.

In a society where children and parents face all kinds of pressures and dangers, we recognise that it takes more than one or two people to ensure that a child grows up in love and security; that we all share a responsibility towards the children of others and to one another; and our presence here is a recognition of that commitment.

All: Welcome into our hearts and into our lives.

In a world where adults want children to grow up in their own image, we recognise that we can only provide our love and support, while our children create their own lives – their own futures.

All: Welcome into our hearts and into our lives.

We recognise, too, that we have much to learn from our children, who teach us every day about love, trust, honesty, fun, the excitement of learning, and the importance of play.

All: Welcome into our hearts and into our lives.

In a world where there is much hurt and many broken dreams, we celebrate the beauty and joy of new life and the wonder, creativity, and intrinsic value of the human spirit.

All: Welcome into our hearts and into our lives.

We give thanks for the many privileges and opportunities we enjoy, particularly the very special privilege of looking on the smiling face of a child, being able to hold him/her in our arms and know the true meaning of love. Amen

Roger Courtney

....

Each new life is a field of unlimited potentiality.
Help us to support this child to achieve his/her potential.

All: Each new life is a blessing and a joy.

Each new life calls us to be the best that we can be in supporting, guiding, and protecting them.
Help us to step up to the mark.

All: Each new life is a blessing and a joy.

Each new life has to make its own way to eventual independence.
Help us to love in a way that enables him/her to build a fulfilling life independent of us.

All: Each new life is a blessing and a joy.

Roger Courtney

....

Closing words

This is a day of celebration.
Let it also be a day of dedication.
The world does a good job of reminding us how fragile we are.
Every child needs the love, nurture, and support
of a network of family and friends.
On this special day, in a few moments of silence that follow,
I ask each of us, in our own way,
to confer a silent prayer, blessing, wish, or hope on this child.

[silence]

May the source of love touch and bless [NAME] and grace their life with warmth and courage.

Jopie Boeke

••

In Africa they say that it takes a whole village to raise a child. It can be a deeply challenging task, as well as rewarding, for a parent. Let us commit to doing what each of us can to provide support and care for this beautiful baby and the family; and to be there when we are needed. Amen

Roger Courtney

••

Annex B: Words for Weddings

Opening words

Dear friends and family: out of love and affection for X and Y we have gathered together today to witness and bless the vows and commitment that they will share with each other and will unite them today in marriage. To this moment they bring the fullness of their hearts as a treasure to share with one another. They bring the dreams and hopes which will hold them together in a special bond. They each bring their own unique personality, experiences, gifts, and circle of friends and family, and they will continue to build a shared life together. We rejoice with them in this outward symbol of the union of their hearts and minds, a union created from friendship, equality, respect and, most of all, of love.

I know that they very much value the effort that you have all made to be with them here on their very special day. Your role is also important in supporting their life together, whatever it may bring.

Roger Courtney

....

We bring into this sacred space our deepest moments.
Such a moment is this one, when two soul-mates have become partners for life.
They have vowed to take each other in good times and in bad, for better, for worse.
Life is not always straightforward.
It has twists and turns, heights and depths, sorrow and joy, cloudless skies and muddy patches.

Marriage brings us together quite uniquely.

Every marriage is unique.

It draws into itself all that is special about the two people most intimately involved.

There isn't another marriage quite like this one, and there never will be.

Uniqueness cannot be copied.

There are many aspects of marriage, but central to it all is our commitment to each other.

Penny Johnson

Prayer

Loving God,
guardian of life's thresholds,
be with us now in this holy place,
where love is affirmed and blessed.

Caring God,
watcher of our passing days,
help us in these sacred moments
to see the divine in the ordinary.

May we be humbled
in the presence of faith and trust,
may we be strengthened
in love and compassion.
May the vows of A & B,
and our own vows,
here be refreshed and renewed,
and may we be glad
of our presence here today.
Amen.

Celia Midgley

Responsive prayer

Today we celebrate love. All kinds of love.

In our relationship with those with whom we share a romantic love
All: Help us to love unselfishly, with compassion and kindness.

In our relationship with our family members
All: Help us to love unselfishly with compassion and kindness.

In our relationship with our friends
All: Help us to love unselfishly with compassion and kindness.

In our relationships with members of our own and those of other faiths and denominations
All: Help us to love unselfishly with compassion and kindness.

In our relationship with colleagues at work and our neighbours at home
All: Help us to love unselfishly with compassion and kindness.

In our relationships with those we find it hard to like, let alone love
All: Help us to love unselfishly with compassion and kindness.

Roger Courtney

Poems

The Vine of Love
"Thou hast kept the good wine until now." (The Gospel of John 2:10)

Love brings us here,
the love that lives
and grows in two
human souls.

Love is like a seed
that is sown and
which germinates
in mutual attraction.

It is like springtime
growth, erupting in
the bright passion of
youth, the youthfulness
of passion.

It faces unforeseen obstacles,
it must overcome tests and challenges
and threatening blights.

It finds new shafts of light
to draw it upwards, new sources
of nourishment with its deepening roots.

It bears new fruits and, with care,
yields a rich harvest …

Love grows old as fine wine
grows old, subtle in its
flavours, its colours; mellow
and yet still intoxicating!

We give thanks for love and
raise a glass to loving union.

Cliff Reed

....

What if I died tonight – dear God –
Who would there be to tell the world
This man was all in all to me?
This man would have to claim
That which would hardly be believed,
So tall a tale of love he'd tell.

I have a song to sing, my love, a song
Of such unbounded happiness that,
Even if I didn't die, eternity'd be too short
To hear it to the end. I mean, of course,
Our love, such love that we can never tire
Of going in for yet another sure and certain
Bid for prizes which no National Lottery
Will ever deliver, no, not even once a week
But which you and I have won and will go on enjoying
As winners in the precious game of life.

Peter Sampson
(First published by the Unitarian General Assembly Worship Committee in *Green and Dying* (1990))

....

Sand and Glass Box Ceremony

You will need:

- Two glass vessels filled with sand. Each vessel may contain sand of a different colour, or collected from places which are meaningful to the people involved.
- A larger glass vessel into which all the sand will be poured.

Glass is a bit of a paradox – a bit like a marriage!

Glass is made by heating sand (to 1700°C!) until it turns into a liquid. When it cools, it undergoes a complete transformation, but it never quite sets into a solid. It has some of the crystalline order of a solid, and some of the molecular randomness of a liquid. It can be strong enough to protect us, but it shatters with incredible ease. It is made from opaque sand, yet it is completely transparent.

When two people enter into the covenanted relationship of marriage, they commit to transform themselves in ways which will make them both stronger and more vulnerable; and to become transparent to each other in the deep things of life.

Grains of sand have been transformed to make this vessel. The sands of time can remind us of eternal love and of our mortality. Today A and B have chosen to represent their love for each other in this short ritual using sand and glass.

A and B, today you enter into a sacred covenant, joining your separate lives together. These two separate vessels of sand symbolise your separate lives, separate families, and separate sets of friends. They represent all that you are, and all that you will ever be as an individual. They also represent your life before this, your wedding day.

A pours half of their sand into the larger vessel

This sand represents all the decisions, actions, and events that helped to shape you into the unique individual that you are today.

B pours half of their sand into the larger vessel

This sand represents all the decisions, actions, and events that helped to shape you into the unique individual that you are today.

As B and A now pour the remainder of the sand together, the individual portions of sand will no longer exist, but will be joined together as one. Just as these grains of sand can never be separated and poured again into the individual containers, so you must work to ensure that your marriage will be.

Maud Robinson

....

Closing words

This is a day of celebration.
Let it also be a day of dedication.
The world does a good job of reminding us how fragile we are.
Every marriage needs the love, nurture, and support
of a network of family and friends.
On this special day, in a few moments of silence that follow,
I ask each of us, in our own way,
to confer a silent prayer, blessing, wish or hope on this couple.

[silence]

May the source of love touch and bless *X and Y* and grace their life with warmth and courage.

Jopie Boeke

Annex C:
Words for Funerals

Prayers

Let us be quiet in our hearts as is
the still cormorant watching from the sunlit rock,
the tranquil sea fret stealing over the water,
the gentle wave caressing the shingle,
the sea campion motionless in her gown of white.
For these are the mute harbingers of a loving God
and the promise of His peace.

Naomi Linnell

Spirit of Life and Love,
In this time of loss and sadness
We come together as a community
To mark the end of the days of X,
To honour and celebrate his/her life,
To mourn his/her passing,
To hold his/her loved ones in their grief,
And to find strength from one another
for the days ahead,
In which s/he will no longer be present.
May our time together help us
To accept the mystery
Of life and death,
And to go forth from this place,
consoled and strengthened. Amen

Sue Woolley

....

Today we come together with heavy hearts and a deep sense of loss. Each of us will be responding to this loss in different ways. For some of us, tears are the only way we can respond to what has happened; for others we respond more internally, without tears. Some people like to be alone to try and deal with their grief, others welcome the comfort that the sharing of loss brings. None of these responses is better or worse; we all have to deal with it in our own way and bring what comfort and support we can to each other.

Roger Courtney

....

Annex C: Words for Funerals

O God of many names, we come here today, thankful for the many blessings which life has brought us.

As family and friends of [NAME], we are particularly conscious of our togetherness in bereavement. We sense the loss that each of us feels, the very large, unfilled hole left by the death of...............

We recall his/her kindness and generosity; his/her love and affection, his/her lasting legacy to us of an example of how to live and how to die.

We cannot know the private grief experienced by any one of us, but we can hold each other tightly, offer each other a hug, remember him/her often, talk of ....'s influence on us, and ensure that he/she will always remain firmly within our circle of love and friendship.
Amen

Penny Johnson

....

God of four seasons,
Soul of day and night,
Spirit of high tide and low tide,
Life-force of struggle and peace, pain and joy,
Help us to understand and respect death
As we seek to explore life.
God of four seasons,
Help us accept the never-ending cycle of birth and death,
And the growing and the striving and the hurting,
And the hoping and the harvesting and the embracing.
Guide us through Winter, Spring, Summer, and Autumn
Amen

John Harley

....

Here in this place of passing,
we bow our heads in sorrow,
in celebration and in thankfulness –
in sorrow, for the pain of separation, the ache of absence,
and the heaviness of mourning;
in celebration, for a life lived and a story to be told;
in thankfulness for this life that touched our lives,
beckoning us here today.

At this point of parting
we offer our fragile selves
at the altar of healing and compassion.
May we hold one another in love,
may we share moments of remembering,
and may we ever affirm life
for all its pain
in all its glory.
Amen

Celia Midgley

Responsive prayers

Those who cared for, nurtured, and protected us
All: They are always with us.

Those who have loved us unselfishly
All: They are always with us.

Those we have loved deeply
All: They are always with us.

Those who have inspired us to greater things
All: They are always with us.

Those who have listened to us when we were struggling and helped to guide us on the right track
All: They are always with us.

Those who shared their wisdom with us and enabled us to see more of the truth
All: They are always with us.

Those to whom we have had to say goodbye with great sadness
All: They are always with us.

Roger Courtney

....

Those who have given so much joy to the world
All: We are now their hands and hearts.

Those who gave unselfishly to others
All: We are now their hands and hearts.

Those who were so much part of our lives
All: We are now their hands and hearts.

Those who made us who we are
All: We are now their hands and hearts.

Let us live up to the hopes they had for us
All: We are now their hands and hearts.

Roger Courtney

....

Prayer for one who died alone and unknown

We gather for the funeral of 'John Smith', who died alone in his flat. Advertisements were placed in the press of this town and adjoining towns, but there has been no response. In his flat there was nothing to connect him with any other person, no photographs, letters, or old documents. He has been a tenant of the council for the last fifteen years.

Today we stand on behalf of all the people who ever knew him, who would be sad if they knew about his death. We represent the family members he was brought up with. We represent partners and children that he might have had but has lost contact with. We stand for colleagues he once worked with, and we stand for his lost friends.

In this service we commit his spirit to God's care in the certainty that every soul returns to the love of God. We pray that all those we are standing for here will have memories of him that from time to time will arise and make them smile and then wonder where he is. We pray that his name will come up in conversations, and that he is not entirely forgotten.

We pray that in his flat he had good memories to nourish the hours he spent alone, and that he had found peace in his heart.

In our prayer we close the accounts of his life. If there is anger or hurt associated with the memory of his name, may it turn to understanding and forgiveness. May all who ever knew him be reconciled to his absence from their lives.

We will return his body to the elements from which all life comes. We give him our blessings.

Tony McNeile

Prayer for one who left her body to scientific research

Friends, we have gathered here today
To bid farewell to XXX.
Here we have celebrated her life,
Given thanks for all she meant to us.

Let us now commit her life to our memory,
As she committed her body to help the living.
May we honour her gift.
May her spirit live on ...
In us

Celia Cartwright

....

Poems

The Time of Dissolution

To live in this world
you must be able
to do three things:
to love what is mortal;
to hold it
against your bones knowing
your own life depends on it;
and, when the time comes to let it go,
to let it go.

Mary Oliver, from 'In Blackwater Woods' (1983)

....

In this time of dissolution
be with us, Spirit of wholeness
and restoration.

This is the time of the body's
dissolution, the breaking of
the physical bonds that once
were living sinews.

This is the time of the self's
dissolution, the fragmentation
of the construct that once was
consciousness and reason,
awareness, mind and reflection.

This is the time of dissolution,
of the soul's flight,
of personality's fading,
of the end of active
participation in this
material world.

This is the time of dissolution,
the time to let go of what cannot
be held on to –
but our memory remains
and our love.
These we give thanks for.
We cherish them as part of our whole selves
and in cherishing them our wholeness is restored.

Cliff Reed

Peace After Suffering

God of our hearts,
bringer of comfort when we
think no comfort can be found,
be with all who mourn today.

Giver of peace after suffering,
we thank you for the final gift
you give us, and which you have
granted to our dear *sister/brother*...

Help us bear grief's burden,
to bear each other's burdens,
and to find joy in our memories.
May it be so. Amen.

Cliff Reed

Why Remember?

Is it futile to remember
Those you have lost?

Those whose love once
Filled your life with joy?

Those you will never see again,
Can never see again?

Is it futile to remember them
When it brings such sorrow?

No, it's not.

The pain of remembering
is worth it.

In remembrance they live again
In our hearts.

Their faces, voices, movement
Arise from the deeps of memory.

They brighten our present, even
Though tears may flow.

Something remains.
All is not lost.
Remember.

Cliff Reed

....

Closing Words

We leave this place of sadness today, knowing that the love that was shared with us will never leave. So let us leave in celebration of a very special life which has made its mark on all of us. Go in peace. Amen

Roger Courtney

Annex D: Words for a Membership Service

Call to Worship

Here within these old stone walls, *(NB change as appropriate)*
Here in this sanctuary of love and justice,
We pause in our busy lives
To consider what is worthy of our deepest yearnings.
In the time we are given here,
May we grieve for what is lost,
May we be grateful
For our life on this beautiful earth, and
May we prepare ourselves
For the work love calls us to do.
Just as we are, may we be the beloved community.

Bob Janis-Dillon

Poem for a membership service

I look at the people I pass in the street
And I want to ask them questions, like
Why don't you come to our church,
    and we'll greet
You and make you feel welcome
    and at home.
We'll spend some time together
    in silence and song
And we'll share some ideas that we have.
God is around us, within us, and long
Is the journey that we've embarked on.
Now that you've ventured,
    we hope that you'll stay
And soon you'll feel safe saying yes to
Experience of life growing richer each day
With friends who have held out a hand.

Peter Sampson
(First published by the Unitarian General Assembly Worship Committee in *A Fair Field Full of Folk* (1997))

A prayer for the congregation and building

Eternal Spirit, we give thanks for the many blessings which you have bestowed on this congregation over many years. If these walls could speak, they would tell us of the countless triumphs of the human spirit, of courage, of strength, of human capacity to rise to great heights, of ability to carry on when carrying on was almost impossible, of brilliant sermons, and wonderful ministry. These walls would also speak of disappointment, failure, weakness and loss, of human frailty.

A congregation is made up of all kinds of people, with different qualities, values and abilities, many different kinds of aspirations, needs, problems, and concerns, but with a common thread, all with a wish to be part of this community, and to give of themselves; to use their gifts wisely and well for the good of all; to develop them in accordance with the highest they know. Everyone takes something from it, and everyone gives something to it.

If these walls could speak, they would tell us of many comings and goings, many births and deaths; they would speak of differences in the shape and content of sermons, and in varying forms of worship as the years go by.

We are thankful to everyone who has faithfully continued to pass down to us, through the ages, their inspiration. Let us be glad for the fun we enjoy together in this wonderful community here at *(name of Church/Chapel)*. We have so much to celebrate. Amen

Penny Johnson

Becoming a member

Becoming a member is a process.
It is a way of becoming.
This moment celebrates a commitment and it is a point
on the way of becoming.

Beliefs, like-minded people, feeling comfortable with
these new friends may have guided you to this point.

Now begin to absorb the stories of this congregation,
stories told and retold down the generations,
stories of those long gone yet still held dear.

As these stories become your stories
that you too cherish and retell,
You will be welcoming others
to this wonderful community of love.

Celia Midgley

Appendix I: Wedding Checklist

Questions for a couple planning a wedding

1. What are the circumstances of the two: single? married before? free to marry?
2. Why are they getting married?
3. Why choose this chapel? Have they attended a service here?
4. Explain the Unitarian attitude to marriage: a solemn covenant, a sacred covenant, freely entered into. They can help to devise the service.
5. What kind of service? ... religious or religious/humanist? ... formal or not-so-formal? ... Bride to be given away? If so, by whom?
6. They must BOTH go, several months before any intended date, to the Registrar at the local Register office to tell of their intention to wed, and to seek legal permission to do so. They will need to take proof of ID, and documents showing that they are free to marry, that they have residential rights in the UK, and (if either has been married before) a certificate of decree absolute. Phone to ask what documents are needed, and to make an appointment (which can take some time to obtain).
7. The Registrar will publish the notice of intention to marry.
8. The wedding ceremony must be open to the public.
9. The Chapel will provide an Authorised Person (if there is one), or the couple will need to arrange for a visiting Registrar to be present.

10. Full names of the couple and their occupations and contacts.
11. Full names of Best Man and Matron of Honour (if appropriate).
12. They will need two witnesses (adults), whose names should be given to you before the service.
13. Inform them of the fees involved, which should be paid beforehand.

Practical issues for the couple to consider

1. Time of wedding, and whom to invite.
2. Order of Service (will they have it printed?).
3. Choice of hymns.
4. Choice of readings.
5. Music for service: prelude, wedding march, other music?
6. Will they use the chapel organist?
7. One ring or two?
8. Do they want flowers? There will be altar flowers, but do they want more? If to be delivered, when?
9. Ushers: suggest that they hand out copies of the order of service and direct people to seats.
10. Photography: OK for an official photographer to take non-intrusive pictures during the service; otherwise photos should be taken only after the signing of the register, and at the end of the service.
11. Where will the wedding car draw up?
12. Where will guests park?
13. No confetti inside chapel or grounds.

Appendix 2: The Use of Live and Recorded Music in Rites of Passage

The website of Christian Copyright License International offers the following advice:

Music during regular services (Acts of Worship)

Music which is played from a recording or performed live during your regular worship services (Acts of Worship) does not currently require the cover of a licence. This includes all main Sunday services, special services, weddings and funerals. This concession does not include any service where an entry charge is made, civic Christmas carol concerts or any other public performance.

Further Resources

The following list, which is not exhaustive, provides a selection of books that contain formats, readings, and prayers for rites of passage. Some, such as *If Darwin Prayed*, are not specific to rites of passage but might inspire you to write your own prayers, to give each service that you conduct an original and unique perspective, supporting the Unitarian ideal of combining the personal and sacred in community.

Brooks, Jeremy (2001) *Heaven's Morning Breaks: Sensitive and Practical Reflections on Funeral Practice*, KM Publishing

Collins, Nigel (ed.) (2000) *Seasons of Life: Prose and Poems for Secular Ceremonies*, Rationalist Press Association

Hill, Andrew (1993) *Celebrating Life*, London: Lindsey Press

Kingma, Daphne Rose (1995) *Weddings from the Heart: Contemporary and Traditional Ceremonies for an Unforgettable Wedding*, Conari Press

Lang, Virginia and Louise Nayer (2000) *How to Bury a Goldfish and Other Ceremonies and Celebrations for Everyday Life*, Boston: Skinner House Books

Paynter, Neil (ed.) (2011) *50 Great Prayers from the Iona Community*, Glasgow: Wild Goose Publications

Pratt, Andrew and Marjorie Dobson (2008) *Nothing Too Religious*, Peterborough: Inspire

Reed, Cliff (2015) *Carnival of Lamps*, London: Lindsey Press

Sanguin, Bruce (2010) *If Darwin Prayed*, Vancouver: ESC

Seaburg, Carl (ed.) (1968) *Great Occasions*, Boston: Skinner House Books

Searl, Edward (2002) *In Memoriam – A Guide to Modern Funeral and Memorial Services,* Boston: Skinner House Books

Searl, Edward (ed.) (2002) *We Pledge our Hearts,* Boston: Skinner House Books

Searl, Edward (ed.) (2003) *Beyond Absence,* Boston: Skinner House Books

Searl, Edward (ed.) (2006) *Bless this Child,* Boston: Skinner House Books

Taylor, Kate (ed.) (2006) *Marking the Days,* London: Lindsey Press

Twinn, Kenneth (ed.) (1968) *In Life and Death,* London: Lindsey Press

Ward, Hannah and Jennifer Wild (1995) *Human Rites: Worship Resources for an Age of Change,* Continuum International Publishing

Ward, Tess (2012) *Alternative Pastoral Prayers: Liturgies and Blessings for Health and Healing, Beginnings and Endings,* Norwich: Canterbury Press

Watson, Julia (ed.) (2004) *Poems and Readings for Funerals,* London: Penguin Books

Willson, Jayne Wynne (1990) *Funerals Without God: A Practical Guide to Humanist and Non-religious Funeral Ceremonies,* British Humanist Association

York, Sarah (2000) *Remembering Well: Rituals for Celebrating Life and Mourning Death,* Jossey-Bass Inc.

Acknowledgements

This book could not have been completed without the generous support of the Unitarian Ministerial Fellowship, its officers and members. Particular thanks are due to Celia Midgley, Jim Corrigall, and John Harley for their careful and diplomatic handling of editorial issues. I have no doubt that elements of Andrew Hill's *Celebrating Life* have subconsciously contributed to parts of this book.

The case studies presented in this book are real, although the names, locations, and some other details have been changed to protect the privacy of those involved. It has not therefore been possible to attribute the specific case studies to their authors. However, the following ministers provided the basic source material for the case studies:

Ralph Catts	Daniel Costley	Sheena Gabriel
Lewis Connolly	Maria Curtis	Margaret Kirk
Jim Corrigall	Kate Dean	Martin Whitell

Thanks are due to them, and also to the following contributors who provided additional texts in the chapters and annexes for Blessings, Prayers, Chalice Lightings, Vows, and other elements:

Celia Cartwright	Andrew Hill	Celia Midgley
Daniel Costley	Jo James	John Midgley
Roger Courtney	Bob Janis-Dillon	Cliff Reed
Kate Dean	Anna Jarvis	Maud Robinson
Sheena Gabriel	Penny Johnson	Peter Sampson
John Harley	Naomi Linnell	Martin Whitell
Elizabeth Harley	Tony McNeile	Sue Woolley

About the Author

Daniel Costley found Unitarianism while searching for a sacred community that could help to create the wedding service that he and Janet (now his wife) sought. Drawn in to the community beyond the nuptials, he trained at Harris Manchester College, Oxford, and he eventually qualified as a Unitarian minister in 2010. He currently serves the Sevenoaks, Dover, and Tenterden congregations, and is closely involved in the support and training of ministry students. Daniel is also President of the Unitarian Historical Society and Secretary to the General Baptist Assembly. He lives with his family in Kent, and is a keen photographer.

www.ingramcontent.com/pod-product-compliance
Lightning Source LLC
Chambersburg PA
CBHW032123090426
42743CB00007B/443